ALWAYS BEEN THERE

Also by Michael Streissguth

Johnny Cash: The Biography

Johnny Cash at Folsom Prison: The Making of a Masterpiece

Ring of Fire: The Johnny Cash Reader (editor)

Voices of the Country: Interviews with Classic Country Performers

Like a Moth to a Flame: The Jim Reeves Story

Eddy Arnold: Pioneer of the Nashville Sound

ALWAYS BEEN THERE

ROSANNE CASH,
THE LIST,
and the SPIRIT of
SOUTHERN MUSIC

Michael Streissguth

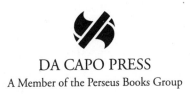

DA CAPO PRESS
A Member of the Perseus Books Group

Designed by Trish Wilkinson
Set in 11.5-point Goudy by The Perseus Books Group

Library of Congress Cataloging-in-Publication Data
Streissguth, Michael.
    Always been there : Rosanne Cash, the List, and the spirit of southern music / Michael Streissguth.—1st Da Capo Press ed.
        p.   cm.
    Includes bibliographical references and index.
    ISBN 978-0-306-81852-3 (alk. paper)
    1. Cash, Rosanne.   2. Singers—United States—Biography.
3. Cash, Rosanne. List.   I. Title.
    ML420.C2654S87 2009
    782.421642092—dc22
    [B]
                                                            2009033830
First Da Capo Press edition 2009

Published by Da Capo Press
A Member of the Perseus Books Group
www.dacapopress.com

Da Capo Press books are available at special discounts for bulk purchases in the U.S. by corporations, institutions, and other organizations. For more information, please contact the Special Markets Department at the Perseus Books Group, 2300 Chestnut Street, Suite 200, Philadelphia, PA 19103, or call (800) 810-4145, ext. 5000, or e-mail special.markets@perseusbooks.com.

10 9 8 7 6 5 4 3 2

Dedication
To Leslie and Cate, Willie, and Emily

Contents

Acknowledgments

So many lists accompany a book about *The List*: to-do lists, set lists, grocery lists, phone lists, lists of questions, lists of expenses, lists of albums to buy, lists of reference books to order. And lists of people to thank.

Leslie Bailey Streissguth, Emily Streissguth, Cate Streissguth, Willie Streissguth, Karl Streissguth, Phil Streissguth, Wayne Stevens, Julie "McDuffin" Grossman, Annette "Talisman" Hogan, Danny Kahn, John Leventhal, Bestor Cram, Rick DePofi and Craig Bishop of New York Noise, Ben Schafer at Da Capo Press, Jim Fitzgerald, Linda LeMura, Janet Hamley Ott, Mike Bailey, Ian Ralfini, Bruce Lundvall, Alanna Nash, Marian MacFarland, Jane Diel, Maria Homewood, Marion Pugh, Phil Cunningham, Sebastian Thewes, Kate Kazeniac Burke, Kevin Hanover, Sue Caulfield, Cisca Schreefel, Russ Tarby, Robert Gordon, Jim Marshall, Alan Mayor, Richard Weize, Joe Lee, Dick Bangham, Maureen Foran-Mocete, Dominic Musacchio, Jesse Beecher, Steve Andreassi, and Cindy Baffa and Giulio Andreassi at the IUP Lodge and Convocation Center in Hoboken, New Jersey. And Rosanne Cash.

CHAPTER 1

Movin' On

In 2007 Rosanne Cash's family, friends, and admirers paused and prayed or crossed their fingers when she announced on her website that she was to have major brain surgery. A fist-sized part of her brain was pushing down on her spine, and doctors planned to cut through her skull to relieve the pressure. The news was cruel and unfair. On the heels of her father's death only four years earlier, the prospect of living without his most legitimate artistic heir or the possibility of her emerging in a sadly diminished state seemed unbearable. The only heartening news was that her condition was benign. Still, the surgery would be long and complicated.

I had only recently come back into contact with Rosanne. Starting in 2005, I had interviewed her four times—three times for a biography about her father and once for a documentary film that I coproduced on his celebrated 1968 show at Folsom Prison, which had yielded the iconic album of the same name. Our May 2007 conversation about Folsom had been the most recent and the most explosive. At first she had refused to participate, but in the middle of the night, not long after I asked her to reconsider, she had been awakened from her sleep by "Folsom Prison Blues" blaring from a passing car and through her open window. She took it as a sign, and I got the interview.

1

It was an earth-shaker. As we talked on camera, she celebrated the rebellion leaping from her father's famous album and bemoaned the prison bad-man image that it cultivated. She even hummed a few bars of "Folsom," but when I asked her about the hope that so many prisoners had invested in him, her face turned to ice. If you've ever seen the cover shot of her *Interiors* album, that's what she looked like. "See, this is what I resist," she said, annoyed. "This is why I don't do this stuff and talk in interviews and participate in this kind of icon-ization and the mythmaking about my dad, because that very thing was so destructive to him. And the projections just keep piling up. It's not just the prisoners. It's the downtrodden, wherever they live, and the people who were seeming to turn it into a religion and making him less than human."

Volumes of feature stories in which she bristled at the mention of her father had already tipped me off that I had to tread lightly where her father was concerned, but my previous interviews that focused strictly on him had covered some pretty jagged terrain without incident. Most notably in an essay for Annie Leibovitz's *American Music* (2003), Rosanne had said that she had learned to graciously share her father. ("He belonged to more than me; he belonged to the world and to the perpetual expression of great art. He was nonlinear.") Nonetheless, her response to what I assumed was a rather pedestrian question revealed her distaste for fueling her father's legend. In her grasp, he was already slippery; drenching him with holy water made him all the more elusive.

Since 1979, when her irresistibly assertive vocal style and liberated lyrical themes first twisted Nashville's arm, not only had she avoided Johnny Cash mythologizing, but she had also rejected comparisons with her father. In press interviews that attempted to make her an acorn on his tall and gnarly oak tree, she bristled. "He makes good music, there's no denying that. But I'm not a carbon copy of him," she protested in one of the first lengthy Rosanne Cash profiles in a national magazine. Ever the dutiful daughter, she never failed to honor her father in the press, but between the lines emerged a woman anxious to cut her own profile in the industry. "He gives me advice sometimes," she added, "but it's more father-daughter advice, and sometimes I take it and sometimes I don't."

Despite the adolescent obstinacy she displayed on the topic of her father thirty years ago, she kept her royal name after marrying her producer Rodney Crowell in 1979 and included "Big River"—a Johnny Cash composition that she performs to this day—on her first album, *Right or Wrong*. If her father was the world's most famous walking contradiction, she wasn't doing a bad job of following in his footsteps.

The flare-up about her father during our Folsom interview dazed me like a left jab, but in our conversation I regained my footing and soon realized that her interview was going to be one of the documentary's most compelling. Her sharp insights and observations injected a scholarly tone, saving the film from the tedious remarks of a bona fide scholar. And, everyone agreed, she glowed. When we reviewed the tape, her face beamed vibrancy and beauty and deep reflection.

That's why word of her surgery stunned me.

It was a reckoning after thirteen years of severe headaches that would come and go. For long stretches, the pain receded, and then it returned like a silence-shattering alarm. By 2005 the headaches had become constant and pervasive. The pain shot down her spine, crippling her step. She regularly developed bronchitis and pneumonia and had difficulty breathing and walking, while her neurologist insisted that unusually strong migraines were her only affliction. "I changed neurologists," she explained, "and in two weeks he found what was wrong. As soon as he saw my MRI he started writing out

In Zurich, 2009.

referrals. He said, 'I can't deal with this; I've only seen two in my career.'"

The MRI revealed that her cerebellum was being crushed and was pressing down on her brain stem because her skull was too small to accommodate it. In an apt analogy that her husband John Leventhal formulated, the cerebellum was supposed to be where North Dakota is, but it was pushed down to the Yucatán Peninsula. To correct this geographical irregularity, she and John chose a surgeon associated with Columbia University Medical Center. "He just kept stressing that this is a really difficult thing and you can't just go in," she says. "So I took a couple of months to prepare. I did hypnosis and these relaxation tapes, all this stuff, this preparation for surgery, so that I walked into the OR that day making jokes with the anesthesiologist. It was good. I felt well prepared, but even as much as he tried to prepare me, I don't think I got how hard it would be because they had to remove part of my skull to let the cerebellum go back up into place."

In preparation, Rosanne had also contacted the famed neurologist Oliver Sacks, known best for his books *Awakenings* and *The Man Who Mistook His Wife for a Hat*, both of which delve into the world of unusual brain conditions. She had met him at a party and admired him. So she wrote him a letter about one of her looming fears: that she would lose her interest in music or her ability to make music. In the note, she described the threat to the cerebellum and referenced Quincy Jones, who before going under for brain surgery supposedly warned the doctor not to take any songs while he was inside.

"Basically, I'm afraid of losing my tunes," she wrote.

In time, she received a typewritten letter back from Sacks, accented with handwritten corrections. "You know your problem is with the cerebellum and my expertise is with the cortex, so I really can't help you," he replied. "These questions are somewhat mystical and you should definitely get an answer to them, but I don't have an answer." In conclusion, he wrote, "I do have an inkling of how important this is to you."

"It was so cool," said Rosanne.

In meetings with her surgeon, it unnerved her when he spoke about the risks of surgery. The game changes when you open the lining of the brain, he told her. Memory loss, seizures, brain swelling, or paralysis can result. He would have to carve out a matchbook-sized portion of her skull to give the cerebellum room to float back into place.

On November 27, 2007, the doctor began the six-hour surgery. He joked later that he'd worn down a drill bit in trying to reach the brain, but when he placed a patch on her skull and stapled the skin on the back of her head together again, there was reason to be hopeful.

MRIs taken shortly after showed that the cerebellum had moved back to North Dakota, although the surgery was not without its short-term complications. She had developed acute hearing—like a dog's—which transformed street noise and beating drums into an excruciating cacophony. And she experienced other temporary abnormalities. "When John started helping me to walk at the hospital, I could not figure out how you walked up a step. I stood and looked at the step, and he goes, 'You put this foot up first. . . .' It was so complicated to figure out. But that kind of stuff startled me a little bit, and then I noticed my friends would tell me that I would substitute a really odd word for the right word, but they all thought it was really cute."

In a *New York Times* column that Rosanne penned in the spring of 2008, she revealed that after an arduous four months of post-op restoration she was finally regaining a taste for songwriting. She took it as a sign. It was time to explore the noisy world outside again.

A few months after the column appeared, more than a year after my last contact with her, I telephoned Rosanne about the Folsom documentary, and she picked up poolside on Long Island's North Fork. We discussed screening the film as a benefit for a nonprofit she supports and resolved to sit down for tea before the summer was gone.

A few weeks after the phone conversation, I called on her in her New York home and was relieved to see that, in the wake of surgery, she looked great. Her beguiling smile and challenging gaze intact, she told me about her new album project: *The List*.

I remembered *The List*. She had first mentioned it to me in a taxi on the way to the Lower East Side of Manhattan for that Folsom

Prison interview. Despite our earlier interviews, at that point I didn't know her that well and was groping for handles of conversation when she offered that she was working on a "cover album." I groaned inside. "Oh great," I thought. "One of the era's best singer-songwriters going the torch route. What can she do with the great American composers of popular music—Irving Berlin, Cole Porter, and the rest—that Carly Simon and Linda Ronstadt haven't done already? *This* is how she plans to follow *Rules of Travel* and *Black Cadillac*, the two most acclaimed albums of her career?" I smiled and changed the subject. The taxi sped to our destination.

"Ah . . . the cover album," I repeated to myself more than a year later while she poured tea. Then she made it make sense to me. She'd be covering songs from a list of seminal country, gospel, and folk songs that her father had scratched down on a piece of paper decades ago. In 1973, when it appeared to him that she was serious about the music business, he handed her the paper and said, in effect, "These you need to know." This had to be one of the most famous lists ever, like the list of Adrian Messenger or Frank Sinatra's little black book.

Over the years Rosanne had mentioned the list in interviews, and in 2006, when she toured in support of her *Black Cadillac* album, she incorporated the list into her show. "I wrote these narrative pieces that divided up the concerts. So the second narrative piece is about the list because I wanted the show not to just be about *Black Cadillac*, but about my entire musical ancestry and personal ancestry. I said, 'My father made me a list when I was seventeen years old. . . .' So, in that way directly, *The List* project is coming out of *Black Cadillac* because after every single show people would come up to me and go, 'When are you going to post the list?' 'When can I see the list?' 'Where are you going to record the list?'" Evidently, National Public Radio asked to post the list on its website, but she declined.

With her father in London, 1975.

She had some trepidation about the endeavor. "This gets me very close to Dad again," she remarked, echoing long-held concerns. But Bruce Lundvall, the boss of her new label, Manhattan Records, had called her from his vacation and urged her to take up her father's scroll. It's time, he said. Her husband, John, and manager, Danny Kahn, too, were almost begging her to tackle it. "The men were ready for me to do [the album] before I was ready to do it," Rosanne told me. "John and Danny would essentially be on the road, like the three of us, and they would be deep in conversation about what I should do. . . . Luckily, I have a good sense of humor about it, and it doesn't threaten me really. Sometimes it rankles me because I have seen them—they would deny this—literally forget about me while they are discussing what I should do in my career. But, like I said, I don't feel threatened. I just feel like I know I'm going to do what I want to do anyway." John and Danny probably toasted in a bar somewhere when Rosanne consented to do *The List*. "All of their dreams are coming true," she said.

But the list was missing. From the moment she conceived of the album concept, she'd begun looking in files and drawers, all the obvious places, but the piece of paper eluded her. She fretted that the record label would back off without the marketing hook that the actual list could provide, and she convinced herself that she had hidden it some years back so she couldn't find it, a psychological ploy that would either help her sort out feelings about her father or preserve an undisturbed remnant of him that was exclusively hers.

Perhaps someone had stolen it.

She'd have to find the list. Or she had to channel the list. Or reassemble the list from memory. Or scrap the project.

Now I was hooked. Obviously, *The List* was no torch album. And it would raise and, perhaps, answer intriguing questions tied to Rosanne Cash's life and career. Call it what you may, but she was flirting with returning in a substantial way to country music—the genre she had ruled and refined in the 1980s—after more than a decade of running from Nashville. Why would she look back now? And why would she walk a path so close to her father's? To be sure, she had recorded a few duets with him—the joyful "That's How I Got to Memphis" in 1982 and the heart-wrenching "September When It Comes" in 2003—but to the point of hurting her father's feelings she had often skirted him in the public arena, refusing many of his requests to take the stage with him, pulling her songs out of his publishing company, telling reporters that she was most assuredly on her own journey. After thirty years of navigating around her father's legacy and almost twenty years of muting her country music past, *The List* appeared to be some sort of surrender. It would never be a country album in Nashville's current sense of the word, because husband-producer John Leventhal's arrangements would be appropriately inventive, but it would expose deep and discernible links to a world that she had tried hard to escape. And she was still feeling the effects of major surgery. The enterprise promised to be physically and mentally draining.

From where I stood, it was an irresistible moment, a whirl in a turnstile that might determine her career's new trajectory. In early October 2008, I sent her an e-mail proposing a documentary film. I wasn't accustomed to asking someone's permission to document, but director Bestor Cram and I needed her cooperation, a ticket to her world in order to gauge where she thought the album was taking her and to closely observe the nuts and bolts of record production. I held my breath. For the reasons I described earlier, she very well might have avoided an author who'd written about her father. But on a warm fall morning while I was away in the Hudson Valley with my family, I opened my e-mail on a hotel desktop and read her answer. She would cooperate.

Within a few weeks, Cram and I showed up on Rosanne's doorstep with a camera in tow and shot her discussing the list, searching for the list, and hashing out the album concept with the brass at Manhattan Records: Bruce Lundvall, Ian Ralfini, and Mike Bailey. A promising start, but a troubling economic tide told us we might not sail from port.

We were a year into a recession, but no government man or talking-head economist had the guts to admit it. Cram's various revenue streams were evaporating, and our requests for funding were going unanswered. As the length of the days diminished with the coming of winter, so did the film's prospects.

I began to pursue another form of documentary: this book. On a flight from Amsterdam to Washington, I drafted a proposal, which

John Leventhal in the studio, 2009.

outlined the high points: Rosanne Cash had offered me unprece-dented access to her recording world and opportunity for frank dis-cussion about her place in the ballad tradition, her relationship with the Cash name and legacy, her career priorities, and her quarrel-some former marriage to country music. This was a four- to five-month period in her life that demanded to be preserved.

So I documented. During the unusually cold winter of 2008–2009, I spent countless hours with her, mostly interviewing, but also traveling with her in Europe and observing in the recording studio while inches away she and John Leventhal negotiated the sound and the feeling of the songs that would coalesce into *The List*. Leventhal worried that I would learn too much about the process and, in the eyes of Rosanne's audience and my readers, undercut the mystery and romance of this record making. He had a point. But fortunately, Rosanne calmly and firmly held the door open for me.

To me a bigger concern than Leventhal's was my proximity to my subject. To what extent would my objectivity remain intact? It's a question I have grappled with on other assignments, and as you will see, this endeavor was no exception. Of course, as I tell my students at Le Moyne College in Syracuse, New York, pure objectivity does not exist—everything is processed through our own unique experiences, point of view, and biases. But nonetheless, the pursuit of objectivity is a journalist's necessary burden. So I have the pursuit to offer the reader—as well as disclosure.

I approached Rosanne with the full knowledge that I had first been a fan. Some journalists may frown, but fandom inevitably comes first for every music writer you can name, no matter how hard-bitten and critical he or she might one day become. Before I ever owned a Johnny Cash album, I owned Rosanne Cash's *King's Record Shop*, a smash hit from 1987, and before I ever heard a contemporary Johnny Cash song on the radio, I heard the big, seductive sound of her "Seven Year Ache" in 1981, the cue for scores of men (and boys) across the country to fall in love with her. I suppose I was no exception, although in 1981 she was jockeying with Shelley West and, yes, Louise Mandrell for my affections.

So I proceeded with my mind on the music writers whom I admire, those who splash into their subjects' worlds clutching the life preserver that is their skepticism. Perhaps Rosanne was beckoning me to dangerous shoals, but I could not resist the opportunity to explore her world, her work, and her reflections. So I carried my skepticism under my arm and walked away with a richer understanding of where Rosanne Cash stood during five icy months not so long ago.

There was one obvious question for Rosanne: why do *The List* when the very concept would seem to undermine the wall that delineated

1988.

her from country music and from her father's legacy? Make no mistake, when Rosanne moved from Nashville to New York in the early 1990s, she fashioned a new identity: her songwriting explored complicated emotions in a literary style; she sought out venues for her prose writing; and she commenced an education in the arts and culture that she might have received in university had she not dropped out of Vanderbilt in the late 1970s. Country music heroines just didn't abandon the South for New York. Los Angeles might have been acceptable, but a move to New York challenged the very ethos of country music and would seem to have put a very definite distance between her and her father.

The List repertory—songs originally sung by the country-est of country troubadours, Porter Wagoner, Hank Snow, Willie Nelson, and others—would seem to take her off-script. But in light of her father's death and her recent recordings, which have tilted toward darkness, as well as her surgery, the script is undergoing a rewrite. She's thinking about her legacy, thinking about having some fun on record, and trying to make sense of three decades in the music business. *The List* is a conversation with herself.

It connects her with the music she heard as a child: her mother playing Marty Robbins, Patsy Cline, and Ray Charles's *Modern Sounds in Country Music*, which fused rhythm and blues with the so-called white man's blues. Although she cannot recall her father playing and singing in their home in Casitas Springs, California, his 1965 album *Ballads of the True West* is prominent in her memory. "I just [played] the record over and over and over. For some reason that record really struck me, and I think it laid this template in me for a concept record and that my entire career I've been trying to make a real concept record. I love concept records. . . . I've never really done it. I've never made that kind of concept record. *The List* is as close as I'm going to get to making a concept record."

One could argue that her 2006 album *Black Cadillac* qualified in the concept category, since it considered the losses she had experienced when her father, mother, and stepmother died in the space of two years. Mourning snakes through *Black Cadillac* and through her live performances, which draw liberally from songs on that album. But at least for the moment she seems ready to lighten up the considerable dark streaks that run through her *entire* catalog of writing, not just *Black Cadillac*. "Up until this point my repertoire has been weighted heavily towards the melancholy and loss. There are great exceptions like 'The Wheel,' like 'I Was Watching You,' even though on the surface it's about loss, it's about the survival of love. . . . So, looking at *The List* and what songs I choose to do, John and I have had this discussion about the melancholy songs and not so much in terms of 'Oh, look at the body of your work,' but in

In the studio, 2009.

terms of the balance of this record. How much of it should be these kind of stark, melancholy ballads and how much of it should be the swampy, sexy, upbeat kind of stuff. And I am getting drawn more towards stuff like 'Take These Chains' and 'Big River' and stuff that has more of a liberating feel to it. I could be wrong. It could end up being weighted heavily towards the melancholy because that could just be part of my nature, which it is. So we'll see."

As she flirts with the joyful, *The List* may also be a public reckoning with the distance between her father and her. Those tart comments in the 1980s have given way to mellowing. "I was so defiant: want to do it myself, don't want anybody's help, don't want to be associated, don't want anybody to know that I am related. And I know it hurt him. But I wasn't confident enough or experienced enough [to distance myself from him] gracefully. I was a kid, and I look at [husband] John or other people who had to work for their parents for a short time in their twenties and how they broke away from that to become themselves. I think this is a natural process, just because that [in my case] it played out in public doesn't mean it's unusual. It's really natural. So I ended up giving myself a break about it, but I did feel really bad about it. I didn't ask him for advice until I was in my early forties, and he would never give it unless you asked for it, so I wasted a lot of time not hearing some stuff that was probably good."

So perhaps Johnny Cash's list offers its own advice, and perhaps Rosanne's *List* offers reparation. But if the past is any gauge, cynics will see the album as Rosanne's own appropriation, an exploitation to further her career. "The unintended reactions and people's bizarre interpretations are going to happen no matter what I do," she counters, "so if I spend my time worrying about that I would be paralyzed. You know, I'm sure a lot of people thought that *Black Cadillac* was exploitative, that it was trying to capitalize on my parents' death, which is so insulting. But, you know, I went to Europe when *Black Cadillac* came out, and it so happened that the release of *Black Cadillac* in Europe coincided with the release of the movie [*Walk the Line*] in Europe, and I didn't intend it that way, it just happened, and so of course I was accused of trying to ride the coattails of that. It's so frustrating. But the other day I just happened to see this *New York Times* interview I did when it came out, and they said something about that, and I said, 'Well, you know, am I supposed to stop working because everybody's lost their mind?'"

Such criticism has snagged Rosanne in the past three decades, as have divorce, drug abuse, death, and self-doubt, but for the mo-

In Zurich with Jeff Allen on bass, 2009.

ment, in the winter of 2008–2009, she peers through those thorny bushes with a bead on her musical heritage. The link to that past takes shape in one simple memory, when her father gave a lesson in folk music history to her daughter's kindergarten class. "I was with my chin on my chest because he was so erudite, and he was so coherent about the arc of it. He started with Appalachian and went through protest songs to Delta blues . . . in a kind of linear way. He connected the dots so that all these five- and six-year-olds could understand it. It was unbelievable. I remember sitting there and thinking, 'Why isn't anybody recording this?' It was the first time I ever heard my dad speak extemporaneously and in depth about the history of American music and what it meant to him, particularly southern American music. After he ended it, this little kid raised his hand and said, 'Can you duck walk?' My dad said, 'Well, I don't know.' And he got up and he did it.

"When I think about the list, I think about that day in front of the kindergartners. It is always in the back of my mind that he didn't just jot down this list off the top of his head, that this was something he had really given a lot of thought to and knew a lot about."

CHAPTER 2

Sweet Memories

Autumn sun glosses the wooden door that leads into Rosanne's house, painting an ironic contrast to a cobweb made of black pipe cleaners that dangles from the door frame two weeks after Halloween. Sharp air skips off the Hudson River and dashes down her street.

Inside, Rosanne ponders her father's list. For weeks, she has dug in boxes, opened files, and paged through scrapbooks in search of it. "I looked for the list a long time and even hired somebody to help me look for it," she says wearily. "Had an old filing cabinet unlocked. Found a lot of other stuff that was very emotional. I prayed to find the list, tried to dream of where the list was." Gesturing upward from the main floor where we sit in her old home, she insists that the document lives in the upper room, among her guitars, diaries, long-playing albums, and her father's personal effects.

Rosanne has sifted through papers and books and award citations and revisited the births of her four children, marriages to Rodney Crowell and John Leventhal, parties with her sisters Kathy, Cindy, and Tara, and California visits with her mother Vivian, who died in 2005. She half-expects the list—a burning memory right now—to curl from a turning page or drop out of an income tax file.

"Half-expects" because years ago she remembers finding the piece of paper and stowing it in a box or file that she knew then would be

Searching for the list in the upper room.

difficult to find later. "I hid a nice pair of earrings once," she quips. "I don't know why. I would need a shrink to tell me that." Although a shrink might be helpful in finding the list, Rosanne has instead enlisted the vision of a psychic. In front of her laptop in her kitchen, which is rapidly losing the afternoon light, she calls up an e-mail from her liaison to the dark. The subject heading reads, "My father's missing list." The first line says, "I have an answer for you, but I haven't received your check yet." Rosanne sheepishly explains that she doesn't normally go in for the paranormal, but, she adds, "I had exhausted all the logical avenues. I might as well try something mystical."

Rosanne chuckles and then reads from the instructions. The unnamed clairvoyant tells her that the missing document dwells in a visible place in her home, near a closet that contains water, by a cabinet that contains "little secrets." It may be near a water-damaged space, says the note, and could take fifteen to sixteen months to find. Rosanne points out that leaking water has damaged walls in her upper room and that the bathroom up there might pass for the "closet that contains water." Rising from the laptop, she leads the way upstairs.

In the upper room, her father's silver Halliburton case gleams on a shelf next to a box crammed with letters and cards he mailed to her over the years. Her son Jake's building-block projects rise on a table, and gold records cover the wall. Peering over her reading glasses, Rosanne inspects the built-in shelves that line one of the walls and then turns to a free-standing shelf full of scrapbooks and photo albums. She gingerly pulls one from a stack and opens it. Yellowed newspaper clippings describing the Beatles' breakup mingle with ones about her father's Folsom Prison show in 1968, when she was twelve years old. All of this covers her musical heritage, but no list flutters out of these memories despite their proximity to water-damaged walls. Her hands place the book back on the shelf.

Rosanne allows that sometime earlier in the autumn she may have lost the desire to find the list. "I realized that a part of me didn't want to find the list, that my desperation was partly feigned. So I had to start asking myself why I didn't really want to find the list. It's partly because it's mine. And I feel like everything about my father has been appropriated publicly. Here was something that was as if he was a martial arts guy and I was a student and he was passing it to me. Why should I let the public appropriate it? . . . The feeling of everybody wanting to appropriate it, that's what I was resisting. I had to just step back, just think about it, and re-own it. I think once I really have ownership of it, I'll find it." If the list shows up, part of owning it may mean keeping it from the public's eyes. It's a tactile connection to her father that she will not surrender, unlike his clothing and guitar and passports, which dwell in museums and private collections around the world.

Searching.

Yet the idea of the list—that it symbolizes a chain—keeps her trained on her album project. "The list represents the template of my musicality," she explains, "and it's not fair for it to disappear and stop with me. I have a daughter [Chelsea] who's a musician. She should get to know the list too. If nothing else."

Downstairs, sitting on a soft sofa, the afternoon light all but gone, she picks up the notion of the chain again. "That's thrilling to me to be the next in the line of interpreters. Love it. I'm ready. Sign me up. . . . What I would be uncomfortable with is if it was exploitation, if it was presented in a way that was about my dad: 'Oh, look at this artifact my dad left me. Let me help make him more famous.' And sell myself out in the process. That is why I haven't found the list, because any whiff of that . . . I can't go there.

But when I think about the music and what it means and this opportunity to reinterpret it, to document it, it's part of a lexicon of American music, it's a responsibility and an honor."

Five days into the new year and still no list. Rosanne is undeterred, though. She and John have made a parlor game of imagining songs on the list or songs that might have been on the list, acknowledging that their choices for the album may ultimately rise from the spirit of the list.

And they are not the only musicians thinking about legacy and songs gone by. This winter Steve Earle is recording an album of songs by the late Townes Van Zandt, and Bob Dylan is reworking an old Willie Dixon blues for his *Together Through Life* album. While Earle and Dylan toil, the band Wilco stirs up a cover of Woody Guthrie's hard-times classic "The Jolly Banker," and Elvis Costello puts to bed a new album that rings of traditional country. Pretty soon, in the service of southern music, Jeff Tweedy of Wilco and Costello will lend their vocals to tracks on *The List*.

Rosanne and I stand on Seventh Avenue waiting for John to summon a cab. One might be more persuaded to stop for Rosanne, her blushed face set into the high collar of a stylish winter coat, but hailing cabs seems to be John's responsibility. While we wait, a crisp sun glances off the glass facades of tall buildings and down onto the New Yorkers hustling by, wrapped up against the chilly January winds. My eyes size up a shuttered corner store across the street as a cab finally veers toward the curb. The destination is Gansevoort Street and a studio co-owned by producer, engineer, and John's longtime friend Rick DePofi, where Rosanne will record her album. This morning she's laying down vocal tracks while trying to shake off the remnants of the flu.

All weekend she sat up in bed, propped up on pillows, watching television and e-mailing friends from her laptop, all the while expanding her vision of *The List*. In an e-mail, she told me that she and John had already recorded ten demos of songs that she thinks are on the list, but if they're not on the list, she doesn't want to have to discard them. She mused about doing a second album if the list doesn't show up in time for the first album. "I want to have my cake and eat it too," she wrote, "but this extends the whole project from a single record." I replied that the current album didn't necessarily have to live or die by the actual list and asked her if she really wanted to dedicate such a big chunk of her time to a follow-up just to apologize for not having the list the first time around.

As her fever subsided over the weekend, she contacted me again. "I am now looking forward to talking to you about this project. I really can't wait for you to hear some of this stuff, although it will have to be next time I see you I think. John is being so careful. He only let Danny hear it for the first time last week. But I think you misunderstood about the second *List* record. It wouldn't be as an apology. It would be a follow-up."

On Seventh Avenue, the cab shoots downtown and cuts west to Gansevoort Street. Contrary to her e-mail, she and John have decided not to make me wait to listen. On the way I confess that when I first heard Rosanne say "cover album" back before her surgery, Linda Ronstadt's *Lush Life* came to mind. John jokes that they could pull from Tin Pan Alley's country-and-western efforts: "Don't Fence Me In" and "I'm an Old Cowhand." That reminds me that Dave Brubeck's saxophonist Paul Desmond used to slip into "Don't Fence Me In" onstage whenever Brubeck, a rancher's son, strayed off beat. Picking up the beat, Leventhal offers that Desmond remains one of his favorite jazz musicians, one of the great melodic instrumentalists and a serious student whose New York apartment was lined with books. John mentions that last year he contributed to jazz bassist Charlie Haden's *Rambling Boy* album and brought Rosanne along to add vocals to the Carter Family's "Wildwood Flower." "How'd that album do?" Rosanne chimes in from her side of the taxicab bench. John grins. "It's only the number-one jazz album in the country right now, honey—or close to it."

In the studio, John whistles to himself as he calls up tracks that he has already recorded for Rosanne. This is a demo session, plain and simple, an opportunity to build tracks that will give John, the band, and Rosanne a template when it's time to record final cuts, if these songs make it that far. Songs recorded at this stage may be discarded. John and manager Danny Kahn will also take the demos to Mike Bailey and Ian Ralfini at Manhattan to assure them that all is moving along smoothly. While John whistles, Rosanne wrinkles her nose as she walks through the outside room into the studio.

John.

"I have to say, this studio is now filthier than yours, John." (John has a studio on East Twelfth Street.) Throughout the two demo sessions I attend in the month of January, Rosanne will complain about the foul smell of garbage. I can't disagree with her.

The husband and wife have worked out Ray Price's "I'll Be There (If You Ever Want Me)," a rollicking, shuffling western swing number from 1954 that augured the Cherokee Cowboy's sizzling "Crazy Arms" of 1956. Written by Rusty Gabbard, a former member of Cowboy Copas's band, it hit number two on the country music charts. Price almost certainly made Johnny Cash's list. His records took their place in Cash's collection before the Man in Black ever sang for Sun Records, and he and Marshall Grant and Luther Perkins spun Price's records on their living room turntables in Memphis when they broke from practicing their own music. Sad and amazing to think that the bookends of Cash's career sit inside the ever-expanding arc of Price's: While Cash was still an air force staff sergeant, Price had established himself in the public eye, and today he continues to record and tour five years after Cash's death. Cash never covered a song exclusively linked to Price, but Rosanne takes control of "I'll Be There" on Gansevoort Street. The exuberant beat worms its way into my brain, where it remains all day.

Wearing a black cable-knit sweater and sleek leggings, Rosanne sits on a couch while she sings, a microphone planted in front of her. She reads the lyrics off of a silver computer notebook that bounces in her lap with the insistent western beat. And although her cold has planted a rasp in her throat, the slight growl adds alluring zest. "This is the pleurisy version," she cracks when the song ends.

Even as Rosanne enlivens this old standard, she strays from the original melody, and John wants to pull her back.

"We don't need to do this right now because you're not feeling well," he says, "but we should review the Ray Price version because the melody is kind of specific."

With John leading the way, they parrot the original melody together.

"Is this key right or is it high?" he asks.

"Well, it is going to the bottom of my range," she replies.

"I'm really liking the bottom of your range."

"It's fine. I can stay in tune down there."

As much as her rasp might be a welcome visitor, an insistent cough has cropped up in the wake of "I'll Be There." She sips water and tries to clear it from her throat, but as she and John turn to Mickey Newbury's "Sweet Memories" it continues to nag her.

She ignores it while John sets up the tracks for Newbury's song. Reaching down to her handbag sitting on the floor next to her feet, she pulls out a flier advertising a clothing sale, examines both sides, and drops it back into the bag. It's as if John is bringing the car around from the backyard while she waits for him by the front gate.

"Sweet Memories" is not one of its originator's best known. Newbury wrote it in the 1960s while under contract to Acuff-Rose Music in Nashville, and although it climbed the pop charts with Andy Williams in 1968, his "An American Trilogy" and "Just Dropped In (to See What Condition My Condition Was In)" are better known. Willie Nelson, too, recorded "Sweet Memories" in 1968 during his lost years at RCA Victor, but the first version to hit the country charts came in the voice of duet partners Don Gibson and Dottie West in 1969. Obviously, John and Rosanne are avoiding the predictable songs, opting to delve deeper into the country music catalog when it's more likely that her father had picked a better-known song for his list.

From the outset, Rosanne—using Willie's cover as a template—struggles with "Sweet Memories." I'm actually surprised that she and John are tackling it, as Willie bathed it in every imaginable scent of sadness and regret. It's a tough act to follow. But at one point I hear John tell her that they're trying something that they've never tried before. Certainly, Rosanne has in recent years rarely recorded such direct lyrics. "Sweet Memories" is a simple, wistful visit to the past that clashes with the complicated introspection of Rosanne's songwriting. But I guess that John is referring to Rosanne's vocal performance on the recording. If they follow even a semblance of Willie's original arrangement, Rosanne's voice will be forced to registers where she seldom treads. It's a task that Willie got as easily as one of his golf swings, but Rosanne's piercing lyrics often do the heavy lifting, saving her the chore of stretching her vocal boundaries.

A melancholy piano solo introduces Rosanne, and at first she struggles to follow it. "Start over, John," she pleads. "Honey, I have to own this song or it's not going to work."

"You have to what?"

Lyrics to "Sweet Memories" with Rosanne's things.

"Own it."

"Ordinarily, I would say this is way too sentimental . . ."

"No . . ."

" . . . But I think there's a way to do this that would be poignant instead of overtly over-the-top sentimental, and we just have to find where it is."

"Well, I think pulling out the darkness of it . . ."

"Do you want to try it one more time to see if you can just get through it one time, just for me anyway, so it gets me thinking about ways to do it and whether the keys work. I think the way I'm doing it . . . you need to sort of be a little more on the beat."

"I know I felt that," she replies. "I'm still trying to work my way into it."

The piano rises again into earshot. Rosanne starts but ultimately cannot answer the call.

"I can't find it, John."

John rolls his chair over to Rosanne's couch and sings her through the introduction to the song. "You just got to be more conversational," he urges. "You're dragging it behind the beat. Just be right on the beat, just be conversational about it." They continue to sing together, as he stamps out the beat and leads her through each turn of the melody.

"One more time," he suggests. "We won't push it."

On Gansevoort Street, John emerges as director—a revelation, I'm sure, to no one who has worked with him before. But the producers whose work I know—Chet Atkins and Owen Bradley, for example—let the creative impulses of their artists and their instrumentalists take the lead and focused their efforts on finding the right songs, chiming in only sparingly during three-hour recording sessions. Leventhal, on the other hand, is Scorcese or Hitchcock, searching for the performance inside his actor and coaxing it to the surface.

For the first time, Rosanne makes it all the way through "Sweet Memories," but she's not pleased. "I don't sound very good yet."

"You'll be good. You're singing behind my playing. I got a feeling you'll put on the headphones and you'll be fine."

"Okay."

"I guess my initial take on this would be we're of course trying to keep it stylistically in with everything else. But you know how Randy Newman just does those painfully beautiful ballads on his '70s records?"

"Yes . . . 'Marie,' 'Rider in the Rain' . . . ," inserts Rosanne.

"Just a simple piano, and halfway through it will be a great little string thing. Instead of making it bombastic, I think we should have that kind of . . . "

"That's the way to de-sentimentalize it."

When the piano wells up again, Rosanne seems more certain, ready to walk with it. In the middle of this take, John plays with harmonies, and he and she banter during the instrumental fills, all without derailing Rosanne on her way to concluding another take.

Back out on the street, the session over, Rosanne asks if I mind walking in the uptown direction back to her home. I plan on interviewing her there this afternoon, but before that she wants to stop at a small home decor store to buy a lamp for her daughter, who lives in Nashville. The bitter cold of the morning has subsided, so we march across a convergence of Ninth Avenue, Hudson Street, and West Thirteenth Street that in Europe might count for a plaza but in New York is just another spot for speeding taxicabs to mow down pedestrians. I stumble on the cobblestones and don't know the route she wants to take, so she grabs my arm and leads us firmly onto the sidewalk on the way to her Chelsea neighborhood.

While we walk, we talk about *The List*, and I ask her why the album can't be governed by her own choices, particularly since her father's tally remains lost. Is it the marketing hook she needs? She likes the notion that her own authority could dictate selections from the American oeuvre, but she feels it's important to place herself in the line next to her dad and spirit the songs along from there. Even more appealing is the possibility that her songs will reach audiences who've never heard the songs, who may learn a little about their heritage by listening. "This is American history," she'll remark later. "This lexicon is part of who we are." She'll elaborate later at her kitchen table, but right now we've passed the shop, so we turn on our heels and scan the block in search of the entrance.

The store is crammed with tasteful clocks and lamps and other decorative pieces. Rosanne browses while I examine price tags. "Do you still have that owl lamp?" she asks the clerk. "My daughter was here with me last month, and she liked it. I want to send it to her for her birthday." Immediately, the clerk springs from his chair and shows her the lamp. She admires it and then directs him to wrap and prepare it for shipment. While she gives him her daughter's Nashville address, two other employees peek out from the backroom, obviously aware that somebody they should know has stopped in, but they seem unable to place her. The clerk asks for her name. "I'm Rosanne Cash," she replies. He hesitates. "As in the daughter of Johnny Cash?" he says, finally.

I cringe for her, knowing that she is inescapably identified as such. But she accepts the association. "That's me."

"May I have your address in Nashville in case there are problems with shipping?" he queries. I cringe yet again.

But Rosanne takes it in stride. "Well, I live just around the corner."

The man blushes, and his two coworkers recoil in embarrassment.

On the street, I point out the obvious: that they assume she's a Nashvillian.

"Yes, it happens from time to time. Once I was at the Blue Note nightclub, and somebody there made a big deal about welcoming me to New York. I had to tell him that—at the time—I had lived here for ten years."

Rosanne's voice draws one to what she has to say, even if she's just telling you to make yourself comfortable on her living room sofa while she finishes dressing upstairs. It peels out slowly, increasing in speed and volume until one gets, in unmistakable terms, her point. She rarely pauses or stammers. When answering questions, her mind quickly figures a path to the point you've raised, and then she executes. She may avoid the point, but she knows it's there and she chooses to engage it on her own terms. (You can actually feel her bristle if you tread on delicate subject matter.) Her only hesitation is in the measured opening words of her remarks. It actually harks back to "Sweet Memories" in the studio, when she groped for footing but in time speared a respectable take.

We order lunch from a restaurant that delivers, and I take my place across the table from her. It's cluttered with magazines, to-do lists, and a neat chesslike game with lasers that belongs to Jake, her and John's nine-year-old son. I pick up where she left off in the e-mail sent from her sickbed the previous weekend. Why entertain the possibility of recording two *List* albums?

"I don't know. I guess it's because I am a really structured person, and so something like that, I couldn't fudge it. It had to be exact or not; it had to be either/or. So to do what I think is on the list and really explore that and extrapolate as much as I want, write the liner notes and say, 'To the best of my memory, these songs were on the list.' And 'This is what I think is on the list'—define the list— and then say, 'Damn, "Motherless Children" wasn't on the list, but wasn't it a great recording?'

"It's a trick I play with myself to give me a wider berth to make the record I want to make. It's the same trick I played with myself when I hid the list from myself because, I told you, I clearly remember putting it in a place where I knew I wouldn't find it, like with taxes or children's artwork or letters to dead aunts. And I remember thinking, 'You won't find it, if you put it there.' So it's just a game I'm playing with myself. But to serve a purpose, you know?"

Rosanne wants to make the record she wants to make. That's clear. But to return to the point I began to make on Ninth Avenue, she could just use the license of her own fame and artistry to compile and record a list of songs.

"I could do that," she replies, "but number one, I like the idea of stopping it at 1973, when the list was made. That's really important to me, and so that in itself is definitely from the list, because it was made in 1973. So there's nothing after that. So I could arbitrarily say, 'I'm going to choose songs that stop in 1973, but then I am into the territory of the governing principle of the list . . . which is that my dad, being at the fulcrum of music that he was and the great artist that he was, having the mind of a great artist and having the synthesis of Appalachian and Delta blues and country in him and folk, that his list is of so much value it would be criminal not to acknowledge it, and more than acknowledge it, but put it on a pedestal. I mean, if Bob Dylan gave the list of the most important folk songs, wouldn't you want to know? Or if Frank Sinatra gave you the list of the one hundred classic [popular songs] from his mind, from his sensibility, from who he was. . . . The list has an authority, and I'm not willing to . . . well, I'm not stupid . . . I'm not willing to go, 'Oh, thanks, Dad, but let me just do my own thing here.' I can do both.

"I can make my own list, I could. But first let me do this generational thing, where we take his list and interpret it. The interpretation is really important. It's not just taking the list and kind of doing mimeographs; the interpretation is where I take my own authority into it. At some point, I may make my own list."

Indeed, she begins to do just that, sifting through the artists she and John have considered for *The List*—Jimmie Rodgers, Lefty Frizzell, Sister Rosetta Tharpe, Don Gibson—and weighing their songs that she could interpret best with their songs that may have appeared on her father's list. "Clearly, Hank Williams was on the list. Which song was it? . . . Well, it was probably 'I'm So Lonesome I Could Cry.' So we did it. I didn't play it for you today, but we did it. John is not convinced, because he thinks it's so overdone, but that may be the one song on the list, even though it's been done so many times, that I may have to stick to. Because it's Hank Williams.

"And then thinking about Hank Thompson. And John and I were talking the other night about if Waylon had been on the list.

And I don't think so because they had just been roommates before [1973]. Would he have put his roommate, his contemporary, his pal that he'd done drugs with on the list? John was going, 'Well, maybe.' I don't think so, and I'm not even sure about Kris [Kristoffersen]. I'm not sure [Dad] thought he was seasoned enough or had been around enough to be on the list."

I wonder if Hank Thompson would have been on the list. "Wild Side of Life"? Maybe. "Humpty Dumpty Heart"? Doubt it, although in letters home from his air force post in Germany, Cash mentioned buying Thompson's "Rub-a-Dub-Dub." But Kristoffersen seems like a shoe-in. By 1973, Cash was collecting the Rhodes scholar's songs like blueberries. He had swooned over "Sunday Morning Comin' Down" and recorded it, "Me and Bobby McGee," and others.

Although I try to keep these thoughts to myself, Rosanne has invited such input. Mike Bailey, her A&R contact at Manhattan Records, has come forward with his version of the list, and intrigued by the communal exercise, I have e-mailed my own ersatz compilation to her. I even suggest at one point that we should all pool our money and award the pot to whomever guesses the greatest number of selections on the list . . . when it shows up.

Rosanne laughs at the caper, pauses, and looks at me as if to say, "Any more bright ideas?" She is thinking seriously about her selections, and I've just interrupted her.

We return to our other sidewalk topic: *The List* as historical document. This notion appeals. "Bill Riley, my vocal coach, he says . . . he's also a scientist and gives lectures all over the world, and he has this great reputation. He has this book of American folk songs, and whenever I go in to see him he pulls it out and says, 'How do you know this song?' That really stuck with me. 'How do you know this song?' Here's how the book wrote it, but what's the oral tradition, right? So this list is part of an oral tradition to me, in a weird way.

I mean, I know he didn't give me these songs straight out of the hills, but the list itself is oral tradition: to pass it to me in the way that in the hills they would pass along a song, and it would get slightly reinterpreted, so that an Elizabethan song became 'Merry Golden Tree,' and then Aaron Copland did it, you know what I mean? So the list is in that way too.

"But also, when I see Bill, not only does he say that to me, but he knows Pete Seeger and said that Pete told him that I was the repository of this music, of recording it. More than recording it, documenting it. So that excites me; I mean, when it becomes kind of service, that really excites me. If it was just a narcissistic venture, that doesn't interest me, I'm not interested, it makes me anxious. But to put it in a larger context, that is really exciting.

"I know what John keeps talking about: 'Be the singer. Be the singer.' I let him talk about that a lot, and I am a good singer and that's fine, but in the back of my mind I'm thinking about what Bill talks to me about: the repository and how do you know this song and how long have you known it."

Inspired by history, Rosanne offers that she would like to take her father's list to the Smithsonian Museum's music label and produce an album of the original recordings. "I'm kind of a worker bee as far as my work ethic—more than a diva! The work for the work's sake is usually enough for me, and so [I like] the idea of doing this as part of service, because I know these songs, because I am the repository for a lot of these songs, because I have known them my whole life, because a whole generation doesn't know them, because they deserve to be documented, because in fact it is essential that they be documented, because it's as important to who we are as Americans as is the Civil War. So that doing my own version of the list, then getting this kind of archival thing done of the original version . . . I want to do all that, and if I do a second record, great, but if I don't, the archival thing is more important. See, this idea I had originally when I went to Manhattan [Records] was to do three records in a row called *Natural Selection*. The first one would be *The List*; the second one would be songs of southern places; and the third one would be a modern version of [the Nitty Gritty Dirt Band's] *Will the Circle Be Unbroken*, like a community record with different artists. And I still kind of have that idea in the back of my head too."

I have to ask Rosanne about her songwriting. Is it lost in her pursuit of tradition?

"I'm a little nervous about that, all my writing is going into finishing [a memoir I'm writing] right now, so I don't feel too bad about it. I did get nervous the other night. I haven't written a song in a year. . . . I feel like, between production on the record and working on my book, my plate is a little bit full."

A cleaning lady whom Rosanne has hired is scrubbing at the oven and drowning out both of us from time to time. I raise my voice and suggest that putting aside writing in service of her heritage may be part of an evolution. Rosanne narrows her eyes, purses her lips, and cautiously revs up her answer. "That's a good way of looking at it," she ventures. "See, my natural instinct would be to get anxious and say, 'Oh, my God. It's over. I'm never going to write a new song again.' But that's a good way to look at it. To set it aside consciously, so that I can move this forward. I like that idea. It's probably what's happening."

CHAPTER 3

Heartaches by the Number

This is not an ideal time for album making, and everybody knows it. Rosanne and John toil ahead, assuming that when they turn in *The List* there will be a Manhattan Records still standing to accept it. Manhattan lives in a large tent that belongs to EMI, the British-based music giant whose history dates back to the early 1930s. Over the decades, the EMI roster has boasted Frank Sinatra, the Beatles, the Beach Boys, Glen Campbell, Stan Kenton, André Previn, Sir Neville Marriner, and many other stalwart names. Today the company also owns Blue Note Records, which pleases its hungry master with big sellers by Norah Jones and Wynton Marsalis. The Manhattan subsidiary thrives largely thanks to Sarah Brightman and the Celtic Woman franchise whose milk-white *colleens* become ubiquitous on public television during pledge season.

In 2007, facing dramatically declining profits, EMI agreed to be consumed by a private equity group in Great Britain for $4.7 billion. So now a group of investors whose portfolio includes hotels, liquor stores, and waste management runs the storied company that pioneered recorded music's entry into the home. Where Rosanne fits into this corporate mélange remains to be seen.

The List represents the last album on her current contract with EMI. Her relationship with the corporation had begun back in the mid-1990s with the spare and reflective *10 Song Demo*, released on the fabled Capitol imprint. After a long hiatus, enforced in part by the appearance of polyps on her vocal cords, she followed up with *Rules of Travel* in 2003 and *Black Cadillac* in 2006. Rosanne left Capitol when EMI merged the label with Virgin Records to form the Capitol Music Group. She feared that EMI might drop her in the midst of the commotion, but the company dispatched her to Manhattan instead. Smaller boutique labels courted her, and she might have run to them had EMI cut her loose, but she clings to the traditional model of business in the record industry while many of her peers have started their own labels. "It's what I know," she says. "If I went another route, I could probably make more money, but do I really want to get into the record business? No."

She also clings to album making, which would seem to be going the way of typewriting or dialing phone numbers. While Rosanne records demos and listens to instrumental tracks for *The List*, the record industry is reporting that album sales totaled 428.4 million in 2008, down more than 200 million since 2004. Even the nationally broadcast Grammy Awards can't be counted on to heat up sales. Winners this year saw a beleaguered bounce in sales in the days after the show, when in past years they might have expected to see sales skyrocket by hundreds of thousands.

Albums are rapidly becoming an outdated medium, as digital buyers sniff out individual songs for the gargantuan compilations on their MP3 players, those twenty-first-century Disk.Go.Cases. There are twinges of satisfaction in the death of the album and the rise of the single digital download simply because the greedy record industry killed the one-dollar single in the 1980s in order to herd buyers to the more expensive album. People finally grew tired of high prices and album filler and rebelled with their high-powered computers and swift Internet connections. Unfortunately, though, the albums that are more killer than filler appear to be relegated to the now-metaphorical budget bins. In early 2009, Pink Floyd's *Dark Side of the Moon* can be snatched up for a fin on Amazon.com, which is also selling Miles Davis's *In a Silent Way* for the cost of a two-liter bottle of cola. Walk into any Wal-Mart these days and you can walk out with *At Folsom Prison*, *Red-Headed Stranger*, or *What's Going On* for six or seven bucks.

The List as a concept may be gutted by buyers looking for choice tracks, but perhaps the album will draw significant numbers of consumers who like their Rosanne in twelve-track packages. Danny Kahn, Rosanne's manager of twelve years, holds out hope for the choice tracks, which, as in days of old, could be the prelude to the golden commitment, the album sale. "You probably could argue," he says with a gentle intensity, "that there never has been a successful concept album that didn't have special songs that stood out, that got the album noticed.

"We can't necessarily [predict] anything," he admits. "We just have got to try as hard as we can and make some assumptions that are backed up by statistics—that if Rosanne's audience were to hear particular single songs that were exceptional off of this album, that they in all likelihood would still buy the album, because they are a little bit of an older audience. If the record is going to be so successful that it breaks through to newfound fans of all ages, we don't know. They may just digitally download some of the songs that they just feel like having, or if they are that into it and know that the rest of the record has that same feeling to it, they may go and get the album."

As the terrain shifts, disheartening alliances have formed in the music world, casting a new glow on many artists who like to proclaim

Rosanne's long-time manager Danny Kahn.

their loyalty to populist politics and social responsibility. In an effort to maximize their touring, where the real money has always been made anyway, acts have aligned themselves with huge corporate interests—like Front Line Management, which is owned by Ticketmaster, a company drunk on service charges that has now found a way to sell concert tickets twice through its stake in the TicketsNow reseller. In the winter of 2009, there is a serious proposal to merge Ticketmaster and Live Nation, the concert promoter that squires U2, Madonna, and others around the world. In April, the *Boston Globe* is bemoaning the $550 price tag on two U2 concert tickets in section 113 of Gillette Stadium, a taxpayer-subsidized palace whose ticket prices exclude most taxpayers. So while Bono pounds his chest against Third World poverty, he soaks the American consumer and barely peeps as his franchise becomes entangled with the emerging Ticketmaster–Live Nation behemoth. As Rosanne comments in *Black Cadillac*'s "Like Fugitives," *it's a strange new world we live in.*

Despite the upheaval around Rosanne, she seems sanguine about *The List*'s prospects in the marketplace, trusting that Manhattan and Danny will find a way to navigate the new music environment. It's unlikely that she will tour heavily to support the album, so there will be no Live Nation deals in her future. But without those deals, can she ever regain the mass popularity she knew in the 1980s? I'm inclined to think she doesn't care, being happy to embrace vestiges of an old business model and—like Neko Case, Emmylou Harris, and others—inhabit quarters of the music industry that still thrive on a less exploitive business model.

Rosanne's career took off on the wings of a corporate monster. After a hushed first album released in Germany in 1978, her father presented her to Rick Blackburn, head of Columbia Records' Nashville office. In 1978 Columbia was still owned by CBS, the media conglomerate that each year was demanding higher profits from its recording labels. Ironically, just as he introduced his daughter's music to Blackburn, Johnny Cash's profit margins were shrinking, his luster fading in the eyes of the corporate chiefs. Cash invited the executive to his home outside Nashville and played Rosanne's German release for him. "He put the needle down on it, and Rick started listening, and the phone rang and Dad left the room," she says. "And Rick didn't like what he was hearing, so he went over, and he picked the needle up, and he put it on something else, and he really liked what he heard. So if the phone hadn't rung and Dad hadn't left the room, he would have never signed me."

Blackburn probably saw and heard a winning package in Rosanne: beauty, lots of vocal potential, and an irresistible marketing hook in her kinship to Johnny Cash. To put it bluntly, signing Rosanne must have also seemed like a plausible way to keep the Cash franchise in business. To put it even more so, Blackburn got far more than he ever anticipated. He got the woman who, for a few shining years in the 1980s, embodied country music.

With the release of her first two albums—*Right or Wrong* (1979) and *Seven Year Ache* (1981)—the critics placed her somewhere in the concentric circles of the new traditionalist and new country movements, communities that communicated modernity while channeling various elements of country traditions, whether it was instrumental echoes, folk connections, or the genre's lyrical honesty. Steve Earle, Ricky Skaggs, the Judds, and Keith Whitley joined the class. One performer, though, infused the movement and the music with rock-and-roll flavor and post–Vietnam era attitude.

"Rosanne Cash became country music's first modern woman," wrote the *Village Voice* in a 1988 article that also quoted Nashville music executive Tony Brown. "Ten years ago," said Brown, "there was nobody around in country music that the audience wanted to emulate: most artists were overweight, ugly, uncool, and corny. And then came Rose. . . . Rose was as fashionable as a rock star but she came from a blue-blood country heritage. Like, you can drop by her house and even if she's in her housecoat she still looks like she's in style, I mean, Rose is so cool."

Endowed with a core rebelliousness incubated in a home with an absent father and a worried mother, Rosanne brought to her singing and songwriting traces of her determined curiosity, obstreperous teenage classroom behavior, and deviant adolescent experimentation. It was in your face and liberated in the tradition of Loretta Lynn, yet miles away from Lynn's often cartoonish lyricism. Rosanne curled her lip and grabbed your lapels, but she also pouted, cried, and wanted love. "Cash was the rare writer in the '70s who demanded both the independence of feminism and the satisfactions of

Recording *Right or Wrong* in Beverly Hills. Clockwise: Rosanne, drummer John Ware, guitarist Hank DeVito, Brad Hartman, Bronco Newcombe, and bassist Emory Gordy, Jr.

heterosexual romance," wrote Geoffrey Himes. "Those desires often conflict . . . and her determined efforts to resolve that dilemma would make her one of the most interesting singer-songwriters of her generation. A thread running through many of her songs is the refusal to settle for less than both—both the independence and the satisfaction." Her early 1980s compositions "Seven Year Ache," "Hold On," and "Second to None" illustrate Himes's point.

If one had to pick a country music forebear of Rosanne's, it might be Patsy Cline, but Rosanne was too Beatles, Byrds, and Flying Burrito Brothers to be considered a child of country music, even though her parentage suggested exactly that. Plus the influences of singer-songwriters Joni Mitchell, Laura Nyro, Janis Ian, and others who wrote emotionally, introspectively, and in a modern style pulled her away from the country music tradition.

There was one more considerable element in Rosanne's rise to respect and commercial prosperity: Rodney Crowell. Raised to maturity in Emmylou Harris's Hot Band, a breeding ground for new traditionalism, Crowell produced a handful of cuts on Rosanne's German album and then took the helm on four of the next five albums she made for Columbia. They married in 1979. Around Rosanne's seductively terse and pleading vocals, Crowell built a sound that was part eighties pop, part rockabilly retro, part torch, and part outlaw country. The new sound rose in California and migrated to Nashville when the couple moved their family there in 1982.

In the early 1980s, Lacy J. Dalton, Loretta Lynn, Tammy Wynette, Sammi Smith, and other female country vocalists of their generation faltered just as Rosanne accelerated her pace and opened the door for a new generation of smart, lyric-driven women to enter. In Rosanne's wake, artists such as Patty Loveless, Mary Chapin Carpenter, Suzy Bogguss, and Kathy Mattea found their footing in the country music market. "She broke down the stereotype of a country artist for me," Carpenter told *No Depression* magazine in 2003. "That's how I first noticed her. She was making fresh, honest, personal art, and with such exquisite sense of control." From 1981 to 1988, Rosanne topped the country charts ten times, won a Grammy Award for 1985's "I Don't Know Why You Don't Want Me," and wrote the classics "Seven Year Ache," "Blue Moon with Heartache," and "Hold On." Yet she never won a major country music award.

Her most country album of the 1980s was *King's Record Shop*, which was released in 1987. It was also her most successful, spinning off four number-one singles. Perhaps the album was a mea culpa of sorts, a gesture to the country music industry that she had kept at arm's length and whose award factories had ignored her. "Cash's

Rodney Crowell and Rosanne, 1987.

sound is at its fullest," noted a reviewer, "and even on the slower tracks she has more focus and appetence than ever before. She's also a bit more revealing and personal, especially on 'I Don't Have to Crawl,' where the lyrics she sings are deep-cutting and foretelling." Amazingly, the album garnered no trinkets from the industry, despite its remarkable popularity.

As Rosanne's star rose, so did Rodney Crowell's. While *King's Record Shop* sizzled on the charts in 1987 and 1988, his *Diamonds and Dirt* turned on the heat and topped her four number-one hits, setting up Crowell for a years-long run of commercial success just as Rosanne's commercial fire was about to cool. Confoundingly, Rosanne scored just one more top hit after *King's Record Shop* before spinning into a commercial limbo in the early 1990s.

Most would probably say that there was nothing confounding about the slide. By the early 1990s, her increasingly complex song-writing and her determination to let musical and maternal impulses rather than marketing demands dictate her path had driven a wedge between her and Nashville. If Rodney Crowell had colored her work with commercial sensibility up to that point, he was no longer around to lend his sound. In 1991 she moved to New York without him, and they divorced a year later.

Rosanne may have had a larger fan base to help carry her out of her decline had she toured more often, but it wasn't too long after her *Seven Year Ache* in 1981 that the industry figured out that touring soured Rosanne's stomach. Her second album release coincided with her second pregnancy after her first album release had coincided with her first pregnancy. You don't send a pregnant woman on the road, so Rosanne stayed home, happily. She explains, "My manager at the time, Will Botwin, people would commiserate with him all the time: 'Oh, man, it must be tough having her. I'm so sorry, man. Is she going to go out [on tour] this time? Oh, man, I'm really sorry.'"

In a 1998 *New York* essay that she wrote about touring in the summertime, one paragraph embodied her general distaste: "I get lulled into thinking that we're on a kind of vacation. And I get a little happy. Then, two days later, a 4 A.M. call for a 6:30 plane, which will fly us three and a half hours to get to an airport bus to take us to a rental car for a four-and-a-half-hour drive into some godforsaken wilderness where some genius had the foresight to book a folk festival, which I will play that very night and which will pay a significant chunk of my New York State taxes for the coming year

Rosanne in 1987.

(and which I therefore cannot afford to turn down), reminds me that I am most definitely not on vacation, that I am, in fact, in a kind of bizarre rolling hell that only those who have done summer tours can truly appreciate."

So if touring could not halt her skid, perhaps a follow-up album in the vein of *King's Record Shop* would have helped. But that was about as likely as a nationwide tour of honky-tonk bars. *King's*

Record Shop had contained only three songs from her pen—"If You Change Your Mind" (cowritten with guitarist Hank DeVito), "The Real Me," and "Somewhere in Time"—and that was too little for her tastes.

She figured she had accumulated some capital with *King's Record Shop*, and she hoped to spend it on a tour de force that would showcase her songwriting. Her compositions had always shared the bill with other writers on her albums, and Rodney had by and large called the shots from the producer's chair. So she resolved that her next Columbia album would be *her* album: her compositions, her hands on the production wheel. She called it *Interiors*. The album, she said in 1993, marked "a shift in everything: in perspective, in approach, in style even—it was almost primitive in how stripped-down it was. It was very intense. It had the focus and kind of intensity I wanted to work with, up until that point. But always in collaboration with other people, I always hedged it. So more than anything else it was like a workshop for me. It helped me focus my energy and helped me see what I wanted to do as an artist."

It truly was *her* album. She steered away from conventional Nashville production values by preserving the songs' acoustic core and created repertoire that established the prologue to the majestically pensive albums that would come over the next sixteen years. "*Interiors* flies in the face of the happy-ending fairy tales that pass for entertainment in this country," noted *Rolling Stone* at the time. "It is disturbing, and it offers no answers. The record ends with a brief glint of hope, but there's little cause to believe that it can be sustained. It can only be fervently wished that on the strength of this album's achievement, Cash herself finds sufficient reason to keep digging below the surface of our complacencies." Like *Rolling Stone*, most critics nodded in appreciation. Joel Selvin of the *San Francisco Chronicle* called it "the album of her career."

Her record label, too, acknowledged *Interiors*' departure from her and country music's norm, but it stopped there. According to Rosanne, it was the Nashville sales force's refusal to promote the album that limited its chances in the commercial realm. But it was Rosanne's tour de force. Like no other, it bore her mark.

It also ushered in a tumultuous period in her life, one she still measures with considerable resentment. "When I left Nashville, I'd had eleven number-one records, *Billboard* Singles Artist of the Year, I won the [BMI's] Burton Award. I mean, I was doing well there, and I could have stayed, but I was so unhappy with what I was doing. And then I made *Interiors* and I produced it myself and I was so satisfied, spiritually, creatively, in every way, and I delivered it to them and they go, 'We can't do anything with this.' Handshake. I'm out the door. So it took three months to figure it out, but they transferred me to New York. I did the record to death with no way to market it for three, four months. It got nominated for a folk Grammy, which was some kind of vindication for me. But then, you know, [it was] followed by my divorce, by a move to New York right after that. And I went from having a six-thousand-square-foot house and a couple of assistants, maid and a housekeeper and a Range Rover and a five-and-a-half-carat diamond to, within a year, having stoop sales to buy groceries, . . . having this real panic. 'What have I done? I have three kids to raise, and what do I really want to do?' So the girls went to their dad's for the summer, and I sold some silver to buy a plane ticket, and I went to Paris, and I finished my book, *Bodies of Water*, and I wrote that song 'The Summer I Read Collette' where it says, *I sold my silver to get myself there / To a room with a candle up three flights of stairs / That was the summer I let it all go / Filling my body with my heart and my soul.*"

A new world opened to Rosanne in New York. She took up prose writing in earnest, compiling an impressive portfolio that would

Rosanne in Memphis, circa 1990.

include essays published in the *Oxford American*, the *New York Times Magazine*, *Time*, *Esquire*, *Rolling Stone*, *The Nation*, and many other venues. Her liquid wit and wistful turns of phrase translated well to the printed page.

In 1993 she finally turned in another album, *The Wheel*, her farewell to Columbia. Although more accessible than *Interiors*, it, too, paled commercially next to her eighties triumphs, but by then her songwriting was becoming her trademark. The album featured her songs exclusively, which must have made it a trophy in her eyes. "*The Wheel* is about the healing process that occurs after a devastating loss," observed critic Steve Pick, "and though still allowing for subtlety of emotional expression, Cash's songs, by necessity, are more black and white this time. Again and again, she returns to images of fire and ashes, and blatantly compares herself to the rising phoenix in one song. Resorting to such hoary ideas may not make for great poetry, but Cash's fixations do turn into great songs."

The Wheel proved to be another step on the way to songwriting respectability, despite its tepid performance on the country charts. At the time, one journalistic wag who measured Cash's songwriting against Rodney Crowell's more established body of work said that the former wife rendered the former husband "a glib tunesmith by comparison." As satisfying as the acid observation may have been, thanks to *The Wheel*, Rosanne's immediate emotional disentanglement from Crowell was almost complete. The new album had cemented her new relationship with producer-guitarist John Leventhal, a native New Yorker and longtime collaborator with Shawn Colvin who would go on to work with Joan Osbourne, Kim Richey, Kelly Willis, Marc Cohn, and others. In 1992 he had produced and coproduced most of the tracks on Crowell's *Life Is Messy* album.

"I met him when he was working with Rodney on Jim Lauderdale's record [*Planet of Love* in 1991], and they coproduced Jim, and I was familiar with John's work with Shawn Colvin and really wanted to work with him, and I think the first thing we did was this song of mine called 'From the Ashes' that ended up on *The Wheel*. I really liked working with him, and I was intimidated by working with him, but I asked him to coproduce *The Wheel* with me. Actually I asked him to produce it, and he was the one who said we should coproduce it. And we fell in love making that record. He can be hard to work with sometimes, because he is very singular and he's very focused and he doesn't naturally collaborate as a producer particularly, so I think that's been hard for him to learn how to do that, the give-and-take, but he has. He also wasn't as good with vocal sounds in the beginning as he is now. Now he takes a tremendous amount of time and care to get the right mic, to get the right sound. I think it was almost secondary to him at the beginning. He didn't quite get how to bring the voice out. And I don't know that he really got me in the beginning that much. I mean, he thought I was a pretty good songwriter, and I remember just trying to earn his respect. I really wanted his respect, and I think it developed slowly; it's not like he immediately thought I was so great. I think it took him a long while to find out what I did and learn to respect it. . . . Like the fact that I had all these big hits and was this big country star meant absolutely nothing to him.

"I had to prove myself, and he came to see me play at Town Hall when I was on the *Interiors* tour, I remember that. He tells me now that he thought I was great then, but I don't know that he did. It was hard to earn his respect. . . . I think he does respect me tremendously, but we had a little competitive edge with each other for a while. In the studio we would argue; it's a very intense environment sometimes. But we've been working together, let's see, *The Wheel* was made in '93–'94, so. . . ."

Their marriage has produced one son and all or part of four albums.

Their first record together as a married couple was 1996's *10 Song Demo*, which followed Rosanne's New York bohemian lead with its introspective verse and stately instrumentation. In a way, the album, which featured "The Summer I Read Collette," capped Rosanne's transition to New York, reflecting on separation and then submission to an ideal, to love. "Instead of sounding like sprawling, graduate school poetry, Cash's new lyrics have the tight meter and homespun wisdom of old Appalachian ballads," wrote critic Geoffrey Himes. "When she wants to complain about a man who is scared of making a commitment on 'If I Were a Man,' she sings, 'If I were a man, I'd be so sweet / I'd give me everything I need.'" In its darker moments, *10 Song Demo* is a prelude to another uncertain time in her life marked by the long physical decline of her father, beginning in the late 1990s, and the growth of polyps on her vocal cords that prevented her from singing for two years.

The polyps formed while she was pregnant with her son, but disappeared in time after delivery. She recorded 2003's *Rules of Travel*

On the road for *The Wheel* with (l to r) John Leventhal and drummer Dennis McDermott.

when the disappearance of the growths finally liberated her to sing again. It is solidly a John Leventhal production, with funky arrangements and inspired embellishments that liberate Rosanne's songwriting from its darkness and actually make the album sound, dare I say, fun in spots. In one trademark moment, the haunting duet with her father, "September When It Comes," foretells his passing and builds the framework of grief that would dominate her most recent album: 2006's *Black Cadillac*.

Like *Rules of Travel*, *Cadillac* steered her closer to her father's legacy, but in recording *The List* a certain kind of search for him persists.

Clutching her new album project, Rosanne claims to search for a way to transcend the onslaught of technology and attitude of expedience in corporation-dominated music making that accompany the

Internet age. "I see it partly as a way of really digging my heels into some old-school stuff, like some values that I don't see around me much anymore. I was talking about that Songsmith [software] Microsoft sent me, you know? When I edited the book of songwriters' prose [*Songs Without Rhyme*, 2001], I wrote in the foreword that I had this fear that real songwriting was going to be like divining water with a stick, that you would go to visit real songwriting in the Smithsonian or something. So the idea that now people are writing songs without ever learning to play an instrument or having studied who their predecessors were or read great lyrics or understood what makes a great song, much less sit at the knee of a master and learn, it is troubling. *The List* is counterpoint to that kind of thinking about music and songs in general.

"When you think about it, if you moved here from another country and you thought about what it meant to be an American, can you imagine us without the blues or without Appalachian music, without folk music, without country music? I mean, it's so intrinsic. . . . In the same way, how could you think of the Irish without Celtic music? This is our indigenous music.

"If you were in Israel or Scotland, you would go to a pub and you would hear their indigenous music, and it's not just been supplanted by what's on the radio right now, what's popular. But yet in America, I think, people feel like we have to progress out of this into something else. It's a sense of progression rather than claiming it as part of our heritage and who we are and our family and our history and this is us, and if you went to an American pub, you know, we would sit around and these are the songs we would show foreigners, right? Wouldn't that be nice? You wouldn't decry it or disown it because it was old."

"We do that as Americans," I interject. "We shed the European ways. . . ."

" . . . We tear down Penn Station," she continues. "And almost tore down Grand Central, and then somebody goes, 'Hold it, hold it, hold it.' So maybe I'm going, 'Hold it.' You know, it's great, the hip-hop is great, all of this stuff is great, what's her name, that little popular girl, it's all good, but this is where we came from. . . . I want to say, 'Remember this.' It's like part of the family tree. Young people think it's all about them and the future, and then you get middle-aged and you realize you are just the middle of the story, and you get interested in where you came from and who you are. And as Americans, this is where we came from and who we are, this list. You know, there are other lists, the Cole Porter, Americana kind of lists. This is one part of where we came from and who we are."

CHAPTER 4

Sweeter Memories

Ten days after visiting one of Rosanne's demo sessions, I return for another. Only this time the weather has turned excruciatingly frigid. The city's single-digit temperatures and zephyr winds freeze the face and slow the step.

I've parked my car in Hoboken, New Jersey, across the Hudson River from the city. Usually—like on the last demo visit—I crash on a friend's couch in New Jersey's quintessentially rough-and-tumble port turned yuppie enclave, but my friend and his wife have a new baby, so I have good reason to splurge on a chain hotel in Manhattan. Besides, business travel has slowed and the cost of lodging in the city has plunged. After years of $300 to $400 a night in Manhattan—prices out of my reach—I'm not feeling sorry for the hotel industry.

I am feeling sorry for myself in the cold as I make my way to Rosanne's home in the Chelsea neighborhood.

There's a creeping sheen in this area that once prided itself on multiethnic working-class tenacity. Box stores that are a more familiar sight in suburban strip malls hog space along Sixth Avenue; nearby, the legendary Chelsea Hotel on West Twenty-third Street seems an anomaly, remaining, as one writer put it many decades ago, "conspicuous among less venerable facades." Upscale antique shops—one is called Mantiques—dot the blocks, along with expensive bakeries and eateries with names like Chick Pea and Mango. A canine day care whose large picture window invites uninhibited views of its clients at play has to be the most amusing sight in the neighborhood.

If there ever was a clash between the old and new in Chelsea, the new won out years ago. Still, a sense of community remains. Despite the box stores, mom-and-pop enterprises abound. Bakers know the neighbors, restaurateurs greet familiar patrons with a kiss, clerks share wise takes on the daily news with their frequent customers, the local gay community thrives, and corner stores serve as de facto pantries for residents up and down the streets. As wayfarers flow up and down Sixth Avenue on their way to midtown or the financial district and the occasional tourist traipses into a local coffee shop for a rest, the corridors of Chelsea are, to many, hallways in a home.

Like the independent proprietors, the brownstones of Chelsea resist postmodern creep. Holdovers from pre–working class Chelsea, when the bucolic air of an English village still lingered, the buildings exude dignity. Certainly, bankers and artists alike move in and gut the interiors to build their multimedia rooms and re-create south-of-France studios, but the facades remind passersby that a wide streak of graciousness remains in 2009 America.

Rosanne lives in one of those monuments to American grace. Built in the 1850s, its wrought-iron banisters and clay-red stairway lead up to a solid brown door set into an imposing outdoor vestibule. I always feel my heart racing and my lungs constricting as I unclasp her gate and step up to the door. I wish I could be the polished, if not slightly jaded, writer who comes to chat from the *Times* or *Rolling Stone*, as impressed with my own career as I am with hers. But I'm not that guy. I'm the supplicant, looking for a story and always worrying that she'll withhold it from me.

The story's pieces are still taking form when I knock on the door. Rosanne's peering eyes sweep across the door window as she unlocks the door and lets me in. She'll be ready to head down to the studio in a moment. John has gone ahead to set up camp.

I sit down to wait for her. Despite its formal facade, Rosanne's home is happily cluttered. Magazines splayed across a coffee table, a guitar perched on a sitting chair, sheet music haphazardly stacked on a spinet piano, a soft, sat-in couch. There are gestures at grandeur: a royal blue ceiling in the parlor, tall white cabinets and an elegantly distressed tile floor in the kitchen. Marble fireplaces dignify the east wall. And where there used to hang a tinted reproduction of Rosanne's *King's Record Shop* LP now stands a tastefully subdued china cabinet. A massive clock stares down from the back wall of the kitchen.

Red curtains drop to the floor in the front parlor where shelves are crammed with books, including a Margaret Reynolds collection of erotica for women, Edward Robb Ellis's narrative about New York City, many volumes of Da Capo Press's "Best Music Writing" series, and a collection of Collette that waits for summer. Compact discs jostle for space with the books: Rosanne's *The Wheel*; Dylan's *Desire*; *The Best of the Bee Gees, Volume Two*; Van Morrison's *Pay the Devil*. John Leventhal's two Grammys for his work with Shawn Colvin teeter on the shelf space that the books and discs allow.

We catch a taxi on Seventh Avenue and zoom downtown. Cabs these days have aggravating television screens in the back, so I turn it off and we chat about nothing. Well, there is one thing. When talk turns to *The List*, she says that in plain terms it's just time to get an album out to market. "It's been three years," she complains.

At Gansevoort Street, Rosanne sheds her massive sheepskin coat to reveal a cotton sweater that falls down over wool pants. Her black boots with woolen fringes tell it, as if nobody else knows it: that it's cold outside. To warm up her voice, she walks over to the piano and plays and hums. She blows air through her relaxed lips,

In the studio.

which makes a strange trilling sound. While John connects cords and erects mic stands, Rosanne picks up the phone and laughs and chats. "Listen, I'm in the studio, I got to call you back," she says to somebody.

John requests that she turn the phone off during the session.

"Yeah . . . yeaaah," she answers sarcastically. "We can turn it off, yeaaah." She mentions a "hip-hop guy"—her words—who takes calls in the vocal booth during recording.

Should she go to the booth? Yes . . . but John has already set up her spot between the couch and console—like last time. She puts on headphones, and then he takes them off. There are three feet of scratched wooden floor between them.

Check one-two. Check one-two. Check one-two. Check one-two. Rosanne repeats for John as he sets levels.

Today she's standing, her laptop with the lyrics perched on a music stand. For her own benefit, she sings the opening lines to "Sweet Memories." It's unfinished business.

The first time with tape rolling—of course, since it's all digital, there is no tape rolling—she makes it most of the way through before skidding out. She coughs, remnants of the old flu. "Let me do that line again," she says. "I can actually do the whole thing."

"Yeah, do it one more time, and then I'm going to make a suggestion . . . ," he begins.

"Which is? . . ."

" . . . of where to go. I'm not going to say anything yet, so find your way through it. Does the key feel good to you?"

"Yeah. I haven't really gotten inside it yet."

"That's fine," says John as Rosanne hums the melody. "Whether or not we get inside it today is not as essential as you getting comfortable with it and deciding if this is a good thing to do or a good approach. I still think it's an excellent tune to do, and I'm 98 percent sure this is a great approach, because it can really bring out an element that we've never ever tried to do. Let's try again so you can get your sea legs."

Rosanne continues to tune her vocal cords, humming with the deepness of a church organ. John punches up the tracks. He's not playing piano today.

On the second take, she slices through it.

"That's it," concludes John. "It's going to be killer. That was infinitely better."

"Yeah?"

"It's great, baby . . . but I'm thinking . . . "

John stands up and sidles next to Rosanne, who giggles at this entreaty. He wraps his arms around her and nuzzles into her. She's obviously uncomfortable, and so am I, and so is he, but he presses even closer to her and asks her to think about a feeling.

"I'm tempted to do two things. I'm not overthinking this. You can sing this ten times, and I'm not sure we'll get a better sound. Part of me wants to turn your vocal up, so that you'll sing soft. I don't want you to think about doing that because I think you sound much better when you're not thinking about what you're trying to do, when you're just in it.

"But this song really to me works if it's about that universal sense of absolute, utter loss that everybody feels when you lose someone who you love, like a parent, a mother, a father, a lover, a friend. And I know that you can get at that core in this, and that is what this version will allow to happen, some incredibly intimate heartbreak."

John tells her, easing his embrace, that *The List* needs to exude extremes of country music emotion: absolute sadness and buoyant joy. And "Sweet Memories" may be the path to sadness.

"So, basically," she deadpans, "I don't sound sad enough."

He tells her that she's getting close as he slides into his chair and rolls back to the console. "Let's try again."

She goes for a drink of water and comes back wondering if she approached his ideal sound in the first take.

"Hold on, baby doll," he says. "We're ready."

This time he pulls up to the small keyboard in front of the monitor and plays. As Rosanne curls into the song, John plays as if he's onstage, just touching the keys, closing his eyes and swaying his head to the plangent tune. *My world is like a river as dark as it is deep.*

As the take closes, he snaps out of it and bellows his approval.

"Let's do one more," he says. "Just experiment. Feel free. Go crazy."

He's working her to where he wants her: offering advice, encouraging her, praising her, and gently leading her to try again. She complies.

"I'm not sure how to approach those long notes," admits Rosanne. "To really hold them, to drop them, to vibrate them, to make them straight."

John in the studio.

"I don't know either. Let's try different things. I like pushing the extremities. . . . But let's try one more time. I think we have something."

They would like to try again, but Rosanne's laptop battery is dying, so her lyrics are fading. They scramble to find a power cord. Rosanne grabs a yellow pad and scratches out the lyrics. "The artist can't be bothered bringing a power cord," quips John as Rick DePofi walks in with a plug.

Still in a playful state, he turns away from her and back to the computer screen. "This sounds good, hon, our jazz light track."

"Don't say that," pleads Rick.

"Don't say that," repeats Rosanne. "That's one reason I almost nixed this arrangement."

"How about our incredibly sensitive, empathic, deeply soulful track."

"Yeah, that's pretty awesome," says Rick.

"Our wind-through-the-empty-house track . . . ," adds John. "That's what I want this track to sound like: wind through an empty house. That's what it should be like."

Rick hooks up the cord to the laptop and leaves the studio.

And Rosanne stirs up a quiet wind that slips through the dark house.

But still John pushes. Wondering if Rosanne has the phrasing right in the first line, he calls up Willie Nelson's version from his computer files, although there are dozens of others to choose from, by Joan Baez, Etta James, Ray Price. Rosanne suggests finding Anita Carter's version and glances strangely toward me. It startles me, and I want to reply.

But John directs her back to the microphone, where she fiddles with the phrasing in the first line.

"Hey, honey," he remarks, "this key is perfect except every time you have to sing the high G of the first 'Sweet Memories' you're flat. Do you think we should try [a take] down a half-step and see if it frees you up a little bit?"

"Oh," she groans, "it's going to take the body of the song out of my sweet spot."

"Should we just find out?"

"No. Now that you've said that, just let me try to give you one where I'm not flat."

"I still think I'm going to want to try it down just to hear it for me."

"So here we go . . . right before the chorus."

She takes up the high G again to make it nice.

"That was better," he says.

"All you had to tell me was not to sing flat." She laughs. "I thought you wanted that."

He's not laughing. "If you could, make it sweet. If you really want to get down to it, this is a huge moment in the tune. It's a little shrill."

Again, she sings just "sweeeeet memories," working to shake out the shrillness and the flatness.

"That was beautiful," he says. "Give me one more of those."

"Really? Because that G is hard to make round. It's high in my register."

"One more."

And one more she does.

"Okay, good."

"That was a little flat," she says to nobody in particular.

"Well, I got lots of stuff to just listen to."

"Can I just hear it once in the room," she blurts, meaning without headphones.

Ever so sly, John sees the chance to get a take that's down a half-step. "Do you want to try it in another key real quick, and then we'll compare them?"

While John modulates the key on his tracks, Rosanne asks again if he has Anita Carter's "Sweet Memories" stored in his account.

"Uh-uh," he replies.

"I shouldn't listen to her anyway. She had the most perfect vibrato that she could control to the nth degree, and she really showed it off. She could hold a note forever, and the vibrato would never fall apart."

We agree—right along with most of the free world—that Anita was the best singer of all of the Carter sisters. "She said it was because one place she lived when she was little there was a voice teacher upstairs from them, and she heard the voice teacher teaching lessons all day long, so when she was a little girl she just copied

what the voice teacher did. And it gave her an understanding of her own voice that Helen and June never really had."

The mention of Anita turns Rosanne reflective, and when John cues her to sing in the lower key, she hits upon a melancholy quietness that heretofore had eluded her.

"Oh, man, that sounded good," praises John. "You're on the mic, aren't ya?"

"Yes, baby! Are you in B?"

"I'm not telling you anything. You don't know anything but that you're feeling the sadness of whole humanity . . . "

"That's my job."

"You feel the wind blowing through the empty house . . . "

" . . . where love once lived."

"You're damn right that's what you feel, and you got to make me feel that same thing."

Despite their comic relief, John wants from Rosanne a more desperate pain, more than wind through the house, as it turns out. Again, he pushes his chair to her and nuzzles next to her. He wants me to leave the room, but instead I half-turn to the wall. She should envision the death of loved ones, he says, her father's and her mother's. Again, she giggles in discomfort, but he's totally in earnest. "That's how this song works. That's how it's going to work. It's only going to work on that level or else . . . it's just a good singing performance. It only works [if] it's conveying some unquantifiable feeling. Now, we don't have to get deep into it now. It should be about the deepest loss you can feel. Also . . . another idea that I had: one verse should be 'he' and another verse should be 'she.' . . . The first time I heard this song I thought it was about these old guys singing about their childhood and how it's gone and they miss their mothers. I'm almost positive that's what your dad and Willie were thinking about when they heard this song."

"It may take me a while to get to that point of grief."

"Honey, all I wanted to do was spend forty-five minutes on this today. I'm not beating you up. I've given you my whole rap about this thing."

"I may get through . . . "

"One more."

" . . . 26 percent of that feeling."

"One more."

The tears come midway through the next take.

While Rosanne collects her things to leave, John plays me Rosanne's cover of "Silver Wings," Merle Haggard's portrait of lost love flying away into the sunset. *Roaring engines headed somewhere in flight.* Its boozy Muscle Shoals feel gives the song a new life. They hope to duet with Haggard on the final take.

On stage in Zurich, 2009.

Rosanne heaves her winter coat over her shoulders, and we lurch back out into the withering January cold. The tears of "Sweet Memories" a vague memory by lunchtime, Rosanne has just submitted to the *New York Times* an assigned essay on performing at the second Clinton inauguration and wants to send the *Times* a picture of her and the band taken that night to accompany it. But—like the list—she can't find it. Back at her home, she leads me to her third floor, where contractors are remodeling her bathroom. From behind plastic sheets that they've hung to protect Rosanne's valuables from the dust, she pulls down boxes of photos that may hold the inauguration photo.

She fails in her search for her inauguration photo. (It will turn up later in John's collection.) So I button my coat to go, but before I do Rosanne takes a call on her cell phone. Deep worry flashes on her face, and she holds her hand to her mouth. Is it her son . . . or John? A friend is calling with the news that US Airways flight 1549 has just splashed down in the Hudson River with 155 passengers and crew aboard. As that scene unfolds probably no more than two miles away, we dash to her bedroom, where she keeps her television set, and watch the rescue effort. Amazingly, all will survive. It's a burst of sunshine amid the gloomy news of the economy, perhaps a portent of new hope in the Obama years. All I can think about, though, is "Silver Wings." *Roaring engines, headed somewhere in flight.*

The Obama inauguration's convergence with Rosanne's sessions inevitably sparks talk about race and her father and the probable mingling of black and white on the still-hidden list. Johnny Cash embraced the gospel music of Sister Rosetta Tharpe that he probably heard as a child blaring over the Memphis airwaves, so Tharpe's "There Are Strange Things Happening Every Day" and "This Train

Rosanne stumbles upon a map of her father's home state, 2009.

Is Bound for Glory," which he recorded in the 1970s, seem likely candidates for the list. So do a few scattered blues, some of which might come from Alan Lomax's *Blues in the Mississippi Night*, featuring Memphis Slim, Big Bill Broonzy, and Sonny Boy Williamson, one of the only black secular recordings that Cash ever referenced publicly.

Lists by Elvis Presley, Carl Perkins, and Jerry Lee Lewis—his peers in the Million Dollar Quartet—would have been darker in complexion, perhaps because Cash grew up in a government-sponsored colony that barred black people. There was no black part of town, like in Tupelo, Ferriday, and Tiptonville, hometowns to Elvis, Jerry, and Carl, so Cash's southern-bred racism may have been all the more calcified. "I think that both my parents were just too young, and they had grown up in the South," observes Rosanne, "and they didn't really question [bigotry]. There may have been an inkling in both of them that there was something not right about it, or maybe there wasn't even that inkling until after the air force for Dad, as he got to see the wider world. It's interesting that he could separate in his mind, when he was young, but he didn't have any separation about the music."

She speculates that her father and his white Sun Records peers craved the essence of black music, that they knew the B. B. Kings and Bobby Blands and Junior Parkers had something that they did not. "It was so deep," she marvels.

Despite Rosanne's Memphis birth and young adulthood spent in Nashville, she says she's never felt southern. "I respect that part of both my parents' lives and their DNA, and I love the South, and I love southern gentility and the way things are done in the South . . . and the iced tea, the sweet iced tea. But I grew up in southern California from the time I was three, so that's what my imprint is, so in a way it seems exotic. I definitely didn't understand my father's upbringing and what that totally meant until I was well into adulthood."

As she and John work on "Motherless Children," the one song on *The List* that connects strongly with African American tradition, she searches for her elusive inner Memphis, that feel that her birthplace may have granted her. The Carter Family, Ralph Stanley, Roscoe Holcomb, and Dave Van Ronk all recorded "Motherless Children," but bluesmen Son House, Josh White, and Mance Lipscomb owned it. "I'm not stupid enough to think I can have total authenticity doing that, but part of me goes, 'Hey, I was born in Memphis, I want to reclaim that . . . that kind of Delta swampy thing means more to me than the Appalachian stuff. The Appalachian stuff I have a more detached love for, but the Delta thing we are talking about is kind of like a mandate, like a spiritual mandate, like part of my bloodstream.'

"It's like a longing for homeland, something I know without knowing."

The white man's search for the spirit of southern music is as old as the story of a landowner's son slipping down to the slave quarters to hear spirituals and hollers sung in a Sunday's last light, or Jerry Lee Lewis peering through the cracks in the walls of Haney's Big House. And those who still search, whose search has brought enlightenment on race, must feel Wynton Marsalis's truth (expressed in April 2009 at the Kennedy Center) that America has looked to "homegrown arts to make us into one people, to teach us who we are." The election of Barack Obama affirms the spirit of that very sentiment.

His inauguration has Rosanne overflowing with sentiments. Two days into Obama's administration, and I think she is still wishing that she'd attended the Washington inaugural parties. "I was talking to somebody yesterday about why everybody's crying, why everybody cried at the inauguration, why it was so moving. We don't really understand why it's so moving. I think it's because he's a healer and a uniter, and we feel it. He's that synthesis that we so desperately want: half-black, half-white, half-Muslim, half-Christian, Indonesian, American, African. You know what I mean? It's everything. And the synthesis is where the healing is, and on [The List] it's the same thing for me."

CHAPTER 5

Big River

Eight days after the Obama inauguration, and a cold rain lashes down on Gansevoort Street. Last night there was snow, but the thin crust it left on the cobblestone street has turned to gray mush. Pedestrians clamber over icy mounds at sidewalk intersections. Taxicabs race past, unfazed by the slick conditions, splashing dirty water onto pinstriped slacks and blue jean legs that stand too close to the curb.

Just above Greenwich Village, Gansevoort Street cuts straight through Manhattan's meatpacking district on a short but noble dash toward the Hudson River. As far as I know, nobody has slaughtered animals here for decades, but the massive, towering brick buildings that once held sprawling killing floors remain, a reminder that blood-drenched sawdust and factory whistles were once as much symbols of New York as today's Starbucks coffee shops, Duane Reade drugstores, and Prada sunglasses.

Along the Gansevoort side of one of those old slaughterhouses, dented steel doors hide various businesses. It's hard to tell what kind of businesses because no signs announce their activities. An after-hours club? A storage facility? An escort service? In contrast, across the street, commerce carries on without embarrassment: a diner, a furniture store, and—a bit farther up the street toward Ninth Avenue—a trendy French eatery named Pastis. Some know the neighborhood

75

for its Hogs and Heifers bar, where folks go to model their biker wear, sorority girls flash their friends for thrills, and the likes of Julia Roberts and Paul McCartney show up to dance on the bar.

Behind one of the steel doors is a recording studio. Naturally, it is hidden. Nobody is invited to stop in and record a track for his mama, like Elvis Presley did at Sun Records in Memphis. It's a serious studio, yet not so serious that its lease cannot be yanked away. Skyrocketing rents—at this point still impervious to the economic climate and fueled by the popular nightclubs and restaurants in the neighborhood—will spell the end of this studio, or at least the end of its incarnation on Gansevoort Street. Soon, it's a pretty good guess, a shop offering foreign coffee and baked things too pretty to eat or maybe an upscale workout spot will take its place. A portrait of a woman in a head covering stares out from the wall next to the gray door, her expression seemingly oblivious to the studio's certain fate

Inside, the studio buzzes with activity. Like the ubiquitous scaffolding that despite the economy still wraps so many buildings in Manhattan, the framework for Rosanne's session comes together. John Leventhal positions microphones, clears space in the recording booth, and checks levels. Around him, Bestor Cram's documentary film crew members—still hoping for funding at this stage—rush to erect lighting, connect to the studio soundboard, white balance their cameras, and check their own levels. They have littered the hallway that leads from the street entrance to the actual studio with bags and cases of equipment; back and forth they hustle, moving cameras, tripods, and cords. Focused, Leventhal strides to each task while the crew hops around him. It's like an Irish hooley.

To Leventhal, though, it is more hassle than hooley. He rules his studio, needing more than anything to block noise and traffic that will upset his process. But right now, there's nothing but noise and traffic. He's courteous always, helping Dominic Musacchio, the soundman, plug into the main audio source, digging up a cord for Jesse Beecher the cameraman. Still, occasional sarcasm and exasperated sighs betray him. Rightly, he fears that cameras will stiffen *his* actors, Rosanne and a drummer who will be playing along with the tracks, and that the mystery and magic of record making will disappear when it is laid bare for viewers and readers. He will be happy when the day's shooting ends.

Outside in the bleak midwinter, a cab drops Rosanne in front of the dour woman. She limps to the steel door and pulls herself into the hallway. She lifts off an impossibly large and furry hat and glances at the mad scene. Nestling into a soft couch, she pulls out her iPhone (which during breaks will be as constant in her hand as a glass of water) and explains her limp to me. A few days before, she dropped a boiling kettle of water, scalding her right foot. The next evening, while performing with former husband Rodney Crowell at

John at the helm. Bestor Cram with camera.

Lincoln Center's Allen Room, she tortured her foot in the tight shoes she chose to wear. Over the weekend, infection set in.

Will she have to recline on a couch with her microphone and deliver "Miss the Mississippi and You," popularized by Jimmie Rodgers? I'm reminded that the Singing Brakeman, struggling with tuberculosis, needed a couch close to him while on one of his New York sessions, and that Rosanne's father toward the end rested on his studio couch when the day's work drained him.

As it is, Rosanne will forgo the Jimmie Rodgers song today and sits only during her breaks. She takes on Patsy Cline's "She's Got You" instead. John has worked out a groovy arrangement that opens with smart electric piano riffs and rings ever so faintly of Floyd Cramer. The Cramer connection, though, doesn't stick for long; Booker T. Jones poking at Hammond B3 keys seems more like it.

Behind her mic, which sits squarely in the middle of the room and faces John—who's at the board as engineer—Rosanne wraps herself around the groove, rocking toward her entrance to the song.

One of Patsy Cline's greatest performances, "She's Got You" showcased her powerful vocals like no other when it was released in 1962 and established songwriter Hank Cochran's career in Nashville. Sadly, she died in a plane crash within a year of its topping the charts. But Cochran would go on to write a dozen classics, including "Make the World Go Away" and "Don't Touch Me." "It's a list song," observes Rosanne of Cochran's song. *"I've got your picture, I've got your records, I've got your class ring.* And in that way it's kind of perfect, kind of satisfying. The fact that it's content mirroring context is great, but you can kind of hear the songwriter going, 'What else?' What else would she have that he doesn't. It's kind of perfect, the perfect country song."

So a song that makes a list appears on *The List.* Clever. It links to the album. But in a real way it links to Rosanne. One of the foremost female country stars of the 1980s recalling the undisputed country music queen of the early 1960s reveals that *The List* is every bit as much a search for Rosanne Cash's place in the music schema as it is a tribute to her father's sense of history. Up in Rosanne's attic, she had dug out for me a 1996 *New York Times Magazine* piece she wrote on Patsy. It was at the height of the Patsy revival, when the Hollywood biopic *Sweet Dreams* was still fresh in the public's consciousness and the touring stage show *Always . . . Patsy Cline* was hitting the big towns. In the piece, Rosanne's admiration for her forebear was genuine, and it's clear that she understood and related to the pioneer's attitude. "Patsy Cline was wicked and fabulous when both qualities meant something, before they were cheap ideas used to market more flaccid talents. She was a source of fascination, distrust and raw, if hidden, admiration. But not judgment: there was

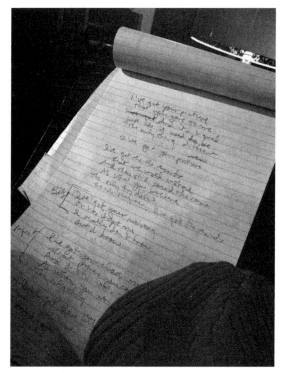

Rosanne's handwritten "She's Got You" lyrics.

nothing to attach judgment to because she, Patsy, did not judge herself." Later in the essay, Rosanne's mother reveals to her that Patsy had visited their home in California when Rosanne was too young to remember. "I sighed wistfully," she wrote. "Somewhere in the blackout of early childhood I had had an encounter with Patsy Cline. I may spend the rest of my life trying to remember it."

Rosanne also failed to remember that Patsy Cline had at least once arrived at her home bruised and battered, and her mother and father had given her refuge. "That sounds really familiar," she remarks when I bring it up. "I remember there being something like that, like a secret, they wouldn't tell us kids what was wrong. It was the same thing when they brought Carl [Perkins], when Dad brought

Carl home and he was just bottomed out on alcohol, like a secret. 'Don't tell the children what's really wrong.'"

Like Perkins, Patsy often toured with Johnny Cash, joining the show for stretches through southern Canada or the upper Midwest. She followed Cash through California too, and one night out there she'd clashed again with a male companion and Cash had carried her home. She stayed around for a few days until she healed. The act of hospitality contradicts the popular perception of the Cashes' California household where we know Rosanne's mother fretted over her drifting husband and Rosanne and her sisters pined for their dad. Indeed, there could be refuge and healing. According to the script, Vivian should have loathed Patsy, who came from the world that was stealing her husband away. "I would have thought that too," admits Rosanne. "There was just something special about Patsy that my mother loved, just loved her. So if my mother felt that way about it, she could forgive anything, she could overlook it. I think all those [resentful] feelings were reserved for June."

In front of the microphone, Rosanne brushes back her hair and digs in. There's no self-consciousness. She's scribbled out the lyrics on a yellow pad of paper, and with bifocals perched on her nose, she gets into the rhythm of the list of "She's Got You." She will screech to a halt when the lines elude her and curse flatness when it creeps in from time to time. But always she returns to battle. Lifting her scarf back up around her neck, she tells John to start over. "Keep the first two verses," she demands. "But let me get this third one."

At times John fails to see what has dissatisfied Rosanne when she stops, but he dutifully begins again with her, punching up the track where she has left it and watching her levels intently as she continues. But it cuts the other way too. According no license to their marriage, he stops her midline. "It's a little shrill. Do it one more time." She heeds him. She will rarely protest. Rosanne trusts John's instincts. She lets him produce and allows him his vision.

This dance will conclude minutes after the noon hour. "She's Got You" is done . . . for today.

Outside the studio, co-owners Rick DePofi and Craig Bishop have set up a comfy atmosphere. Although Rosanne has complained in earlier demo sessions that the place reeks of garbage, today the odor is gone. A kitchen stocked with snacks and drinks that run from soda to well-aged scotch is just a few steps from the soft couches where Rosanne has chosen to rest between songs. One of the owners asks for sandwich orders, but he generally gets muttered responses because everybody—newly free from the studio toil—has fired up their iPhones. It's the new distraction of choice. Five years ago, folks might have crowded out near the portrait of the dour woman for a smoke or dashed around the corner for a beer or a coffee, but this year text messages and voice mails await. Rosanne slips on her glasses and immediately scrolls through e-mails from her daughters in Nashville and from friends around New York. She taps away. Dominic, the sound guy, dashes for a quiet table and locks onto his small screen. The scene is the same all around. Danny Kahn scoops up his laptop and catches up while Bestor gropes for the right buttons to push on his iPhone. The iPhone is new to him, so if he's not careful he may order "an escort for later" rather than a "chessboard for Slater" (his son). How will people not lose their eyesight? Fearing that all will sink into their virtual worlds, I concentrate on the menu—the food menu—and make sure I get my order right.

John remains in the studio, thinking about the songs. Rosanne allows herself to put down the work and immediately shift to iPhone mode, but John will not, and probably cannot, do the same. His focus overwhelms him. He is lost in the session, imagining sounds and testing new instrumental riffs. He devours an old bagel

Danny Kahn chats with Manhattan's Mike Bailey in the studio kitchen.

and slurps down a coffee while staring into the possibilities. When lunch arrives, he emerges to see that an iPhone-distracted friend has ordered him egg salad rather than eggplant, so he tosses the sandwich on the table and stalks back to his work.

In watching John engage this session, I'm reminded of what an RCA Victor promotion man once told me about the chiseled countrypolitan king Eddy Arnold—that if you were immersed in trench warfare, you'd want him as company commander. That's John Leventhal. He is self-possessed, rarely second-guesses himself, and persuades, if not inspires, his men and women to follow. Tall, with massive hands, he could have been the greatest quarterback since Sonny Jurgensen.

Leventhal owns the session, which seems to be the accepted arrangement—at least on this album. The songs come from the pens of others, so Rosanne has pulled back somewhat from debates over arrangements, and frankly her attention has hewed elsewhere lately—to her prose writing and her recovery from brain surgery—which has made it hard to keep up with John. "He likes to work really long hours and then, you know, just go a stretch and finish it. I told him I just can't do that this time. I used to be able to do that too, but not this time, so we talked about breaking up the recording to make it a little easier." Indeed, John has parceled out the work in smaller sections and stays ahead, laying track (or tracks in this context) as the chugging engine behind him follows.

During the break, John conjures up instrumental fills and rhythm patterns that he's bursting to share. In these moments, it is surprising to see that he is unexpectedly warming to the cameras. Like an improvisational actor, he bursts through the wood-framed studio door, banging out rhythm on the guitar, stealing the gathered from their iPhone fog if only for a moment. He picks up a banjo and strolls through the room like Pete Seeger, thumping out a crisp melody. Whether he'd perform so freely were the cameras a million miles away it is difficult to discern, but he has certainly embraced the intrusion in a way unimaginable only a few hours earlier. He grabs a tiny mallet and tings out a tune on a child's xylophone, anything to jar loose some inspiration. The camera loves it. He engages the lens head on.

Putting down the mallet and picking up his handsome Guild guitar, John slips into his swivel chair next to the console and convenes what amounts to a tutorial in arranging and rearranging songs. Arrangements rule Rosanne's *List* sessions, clearing a path for her that honors the classics while imbuing them with freshness, the proverbial "making the song one's own." The scene that follows should be a mandatory course at every school of music.

"Any good creative musician, music maker, arranger, producer, player should have the ability to rethink songs," he says, brushing back his salt-and-pepper locks. "It's certainly something I love doing. It's probably one of my strengths as an arranger, to hear things slightly different and be able to translate it. . . . I'll turn a song inside out. There's nothing I like better really. It's fun. It's challenging.

"The one thing that tends to be sacrosanct is that you need to maintain the melody. You don't want to change the melody. And that's the art of rearranging songs. The melody is the foundation and everything else is up for grabs, whether you change the essential rhythm, change the chord changes, change the types of instruments that you use. Some of these songs we've changed more than others. This Patsy Cline thing: I think if you compared it to the original it would sound reminiscent of the original. Whereas some of them [don't] sound anything like the original. You don't want to rearrange these things to the point where that becomes the focus. You still want the focus to be on the singer and the song."

I ask him if he can arrange "Big River" in the direction of Rosanne's strengths when they turn to it later today. Or is it unrelentingly tied to Johnny Cash? "We thought we should put it in there," he answers. "It's such a great song. Her recollection is that he probably did have it on the list. He probably thought it was a pretty good song too. Lyrically, it's certainly one of his best songs. I think there are a lot of people who may not know that song as opposed to 'Walk the Line' or 'Folsom Prison' or 'Ring of Fire,' which are the more popular songs. But it's a real well-written song. We don't want to do it the way he did it. . . ."

Strumming his guitar, he dives into "Big River," flecking it with bluesy Delta sounds that accent the subject of the song. It's an obvious way to depart from the original but fresh nonetheless because few musicians ever actually stray from the original sound. In diving to the song's core, John demonstrates the proximity of "Big River" to "Hey, Porter," Cash's first hit and another travelogue. The three chords in both songs match—so if Rosanne's vocals fall flat, adds John with a subversive wink, he'll just have her record "Hey, Porter" over the "Big River" instrumental track.

Anxious to extend his bigger point, he offers to rearrange on the spot. "Give me a song," he challenges, cradling his burnished guitar. This is when I know I cannot think quickly on my feet. I know thousands of songs. He knows thousands of songs. Still, nothing comes to mind. "Haggard," I finally offer, knowing that John deeply respects the bard of Bakersfield. "'Working Man Blues,'" I say. It's too easy. There's nothing bluesy about Merle's song, but the title suggests a blues arrangement, which Leventhal creates and unleashes as easily as a fastball. I get the point.

John adds another point, that this album presents a unique arranging challenge because he wants to highlight Rosanne's singing, which is often overshadowed by her songwriting. "She gets involved in the songwriting and the personal nature of the songwriting, but for me part of it is for her to step outside of it and just think about her as a singer. She's never really done that. So in some way I think she never pushed her personal—dare I say—envelope about who she could be as a singer and what she could do as a singer and experiment with various ways of expressing herself as a singer. So I'm just trying to have fun. . . . The record company is like, 'What are you doing? When's it going to be done?' I'm like, 'It's going to be done when it's going to be done.' [My reaction] is in part because of my schedule, but the other part is I want to take plenty of time to really see what she could do and what she wants to do. It's been fun. It's been exciting. We've ended up doing all these things she's never done before . . . , like when she does this Patsy Cline song. I just love it. I just think she was born to sing this kind of stuff. Sometimes I think she veers away from what I think are her natural strengths. I just want to explore and kind of show her like, 'Hey, check this out. Have you ever thought how great you can do when you sing this stuff?'"

It's about time to put some of John's new arrangements to work, but the scene outside near the couch has blossomed since the personal electronic devices were returned to their pockets and cases. Mike Bailey, who is Manhattan's A&R man on *The List*, has dropped by to check progress, and he's chatting in the kitchen with Danny Kahn. Around the couch, it's a clatter of jokes, story swapping, and one-upmanship. Rosanne recalls 1985's *Rhythm and Romance* album, which took a year to produce, she says, because her producer got caught between his bosses at Columbia and the demands of good record making. Dominic can admit to everyone that he has a copy of Rosanne's *Right or Wrong* album cover perched lovingly on a ledge in his Boston office, but he's re-creating the story of the snake charmer, another subject he and Bestor and the crew are documenting; the charmer recently got bitten by a cobra, and Dom is lamenting that it wasn't caught on camera. I can only offer another *List* story. The previous Saturday my wife and I saw a performance of Gilbert and Sullivan's *The Mikado*, and in a karmic flourish the Lord High Executioner shuffled onto the stage in his kimono and zori and reeled off the names of those condemned to die. *I've got them on my list, let none of them be missed.*

The studio combines finally heat up again for "Big River," Johnny Cash's classic song of 1959. Rosanne has sung it forever, recording it thirty years ago for *Right or Wrong* and offering it up onstage from time to time. She likes that it invokes the Mississippi River, a symbol of the Delta influence that she thinks her father meant to acknowledge in his list. The plan is to imbue it in Delta, in a wetland wash that will transform it from the trademark boom-chicka-boom of her father's version to something funkier.

Over the years the song has pulsed in her soul perhaps because Johnny Cash wrote it while he and Rosanne and Vivian and new-born Kathy still lived in Memphis. The elusive lover in "Big River" stops in Memphis on her journey down the long ditch from St. Paul. She just walks up the bluff. Raises a few eyebrows and rolls on down the line. Does Rosanne see herself on that broad Memphis bluff, watching for a father who in the late 1950s was less and less a part of her life?

In 1998 she contributed a short story to a British collection entitled *Blue Lightning* in which she imagines that John Lennon has stumbled into Memphis and met her father outside Sun Records. Again, "Big River" figures importantly as Rosanne uses it to embody the connection between her father and rock and roll as well as the spiritual connection that binds *all* artists. In her fantasy, Lennon and Cash—after requisite visits to Beale Street and an all-black church—call on Luther Perkins, who serves them dinner and then leads them to his living room for what Cash liked to call a "guitar pull." Luther—the accidental minimalist—plugs his Telecaster into his amplifier and strikes an E chord: "John [Lennon] started playing rhythm to him," she wrote, "and after a minute they found a natural groove with each other. Shyly, they would not look at each other, but a slow smile spread over Luther's face as he stared at his feet, and finally Cash joined them on the big Gibson and sang the open-ing line of 'Big River': 'Well, I taught the weeping river how to cry, and I told the clouds how to cover up a clear blue sky. . . . ' A huge grin broke over John Lennon's face and he drifted through the rest of the afternoon and on into the late evening with them . . . im-mersing himself in the feel of the Mississippi Delta and the lone-some fusion of hillbilly and rock and roll."

Rosanne moves into the studio and slides onto the sofa. On the opposite side of the room, drummer Joe Bonadio adjusts his kit and

Rosanne with Rick DePofi. Drummer Joe Bonadio sits in the background. Mike Bailey is obscurd by DePofi.

chats with John about his contributions. I never thought a producer would think of giving direction to a drummer. I'd heard of Dylan's old producer Bob Johnston telling the drummer to put a wallet on the snare to mute it, an amusing and perhaps apocryphal tale, but what else could a producer possibly do to direct a drummer, who's in the band and in the studio to drive the beat? John knows. I'm learning.

John's wife concentrates on the "Big River" arrangement. They had tried a blues-rock version, but Rosanne found that it had forced her to sing the verses in blocks, preventing her from melting them together in her alluring fashion. On the couch, she begins to talk about Creedence Clearwater Revival—she has loved the band's bayou-hypnotic thing since childhood. Creasing her brow, she calls out to John, who has left the drummer, and suggests a dash of CCR. In an instant, John's guitar vibrates with the spirit of *Bayou Country*, and he works that spirit into "Big River." Marrying iconic songs, musical acts, and rhythms reminds me that Snoop Dogg has just produced an album mixing Johnny Cash's vocals with rap and hip-hop rhythms. "Are you kidding?" blurts Rosanne from the couch when I ask if she's heard it. She groans in disbelief. "When are they going to stop?" She presses her hand against her forehead. "Oh, God."

"It's a good idea on paper," says John from the opposite side of the console.

"No, it's not," blurts Rosanne.

"Okay . . . I liked what they did with Elvis on 'A Little Less Conversation.'"

"That's different."

John has cleared out a spacious recording booth that appears to be an occasional storeroom; Rosanne will need to be isolated from the live, throbbing drums. She slips into the CCR arrangement, repeating the opening lines that Lennon and Cash shared in her fanciful story. But "Big River" as "Proud Mary" won't flow. They return to an earlier approach, what Rosanne calls the rock-and-roll style. Like a mother on the porch warily watching her children play, she stands framed by the sound booth entrance and waits for John to reset. This take will point to where the song lives in Rosanne. Sliding into the groove, she bumps and grinds, snaps and glides, scoops up the lyrics and then massages them into a supple reading. Thrusting her body to the beat, she twists her ankle around and around like her father used to do when in the throes of performance. Her body is so at one with the song that she calls to mind not only her father but Ida Cox or Bessie Smith, blues queens who flaunted their talent, sexuality, and mesmerizing control of an audience. Everybody falls into Rosanne and

"You want me to change? . . ."

John's net. The cameramen struggle to steady their shots for the beat, and Rick the engineer reaches out for his flute and adds to the mix a hint of Jethro Tull. The performance is so evocative that I half-expect the studio to metamorphose into a nineteenth-century riverboat ballroom. It reminds me that before the Byrds and the Eagles and the Buffalo Springfield, Johnny Cash and his "Big River" had navigated country and rock and even the blues to a common sheltering overhang on the river's bank.

Back on the couch, resting her foot, Rosanne nuzzles close to John as they let the "Big River" take settle. From across the room, a voice suggests that Rosanne drop "Minnesota" from the line "I met her accidentally in St. Paul, Minnesota." It's Mike Bailey, who says that the state's name sounds like an afterthought. Rosanne glances toward the ceiling, pondering the advice. She softly sings the amended line, which is the only test she needs. Leaning forward, she locks onto Mike: "You want me to change my dad's lyrics?" She's having fun with him. "You want me to change *my dad's* lyrics? . . . That's like changing 'Imagine' or . . . 'Happy Birthday.'" I want to crawl under the console for Mike's sake. By meddling with a classic, he plays to the corporate A&R man stereotype. Although it's an honest lyrical suggestion, it rings of the record company accountant asking to shave two minutes from a song's length to guarantee airplay. The entire studio waits for Mike to retract, but he defends the idea. The matter thuds to the floor, but Rosanne will have the last word. Back in the sound booth one more time, pursuing just one more take, she reaches "St. Paul" and bellows, "MINNESOTA!"

CHAPTER 6

The Willow and the Rose

Tracing Rosanne's connection to each song on *The List* can be as easy as hitting a C note. Or not. I assume that Rosanne remembers encounters with the legends who first recorded many of the chosen songs. Hank Snow and Don Gibson, for example, were still living in the early 1980s as she began her ascent, so naturally she would have bumped into them in country music's back stages and television studios. But as with so many assumptions I make about Rosanne, I am wrong. The surging California girl just never crossed paths with the Hank Snows and Porter Wagoners in their star-spangled outfits. Even among those she had met, few left a big impression.

The mention of Snow, Wagoner, or even Ray Price and Lefty Frizzell—all of whom first made famous songs she is recording for *The List*—elicits little reaction. However, she stands at attention for Patsy Cline and even recorded with Bobby Bare in the early 1980s; those connections are clear, and she easily traces them for me. Don Gibson, too, sparks unrestrained admiration, though she never met him. "His voice," she says, "was the most sensual, round, heartbreaking, sexy voice of all those guys I think."

For years Rosanne has performed "Sea of Heartbreak," which
Gibson hit with in 1961, so there's been little question that it has
a place on her new album, and the fact that her father recorded it
for his 1996 *Unchained* album probably puts it on *his* list, if it turns
up. Though Gibson wrote virtually every hit he recorded—"Oh,
Lonesome Me" and "I Can't Stop Loving You" among them—"Sea
of Heartbreak" came to Nashville courtesy of pop writers Hal David
and Paul Hampton. Still, it's Don Gibson that Rosanne and most
everybody else links to "Sea of Heartbreak."

"I feel inadequate listening to his vocal on 'Sea of Heartbreak,'"
she laments. "And the way he hums at the beginning of it, it's so
authentic and it's so rooted in who he is. It is so great. Don Gibson
is so great. Very different from my dad, you know? His sensuality
wasn't raw like my dad's. . . . I have this feeling that Don Gibson
had this feeling of inspiration about him, but also a little bit dangerous, like he could fall apart at anytime."

I point out that he battled mental illness throughout his life.

"You hear it," she replies, "you hear the freedom. I mean that
sounds callous, but there is a real beauty in that kind of humanity.
Ray Price was a little bit more contrived, like Eddy Arnold."

Of course, Rosanne the songwriter gravitates to the songs, but
her distance from the singers just confirms that although she found
her footing first in the country market, she wasn't necessarily em-
bracing its broad genealogy. She had all the country music genealogy
she needed without going to the Snows and Wagoners and Prices to
look for more. And that was just the Cash genealogy. She was,
through no choice of her own, also caught up in the Carter Family's
swift and wide run through the American musical tradition.

At the Gansevoort session that Bestor Cram filmed, she sang "Bury
Me Under the Weeping Willow Tree" with a passion that rivaled "Big
River." Not a whit bashful in approaching the Carter legend, it was
as if she had sung it all her life. Perhaps she had, because when her

Rosanne with her father in 1988.

father decided to romance June Carter in the early 1960s, a slow tug pulled Rosanne toward the Carter Family, initiating a relationship with country music's seminal family that would become deep and visceral and stolidly inform her reading of "Bury Me Under the Weeping Willow Tree," the very first song the Carter Family ever recorded.

Rosanne's first meaningful encounters with the Carter Family oc-
curred in the early 1970s when she moved to Nashville after high
school graduation to work with her father's troupe, which by then
included his second wife June, June's sisters Helen and Anita, and
Carter matriarch Mother Maybelle. Rosanne cleaned clothes on
the road and in time took the stage as a background vocalist. It was
her apprenticeship.

It was also an experience born of the tragedy of her mother Vivian, who, crippled by Johnny's abandonment, says Rosanne, drove
her to seek out the world of her father and the Carters.

One can't understand how Rosanne so easily slipped into that
world until she tells about life in the decade before her migration
to Nashville.

Her mother and father had met in the early 1950s when he was
stationed at an air force base near her home in San Antonio, Texas,
and for three years, while he was assigned to a radio operator perch
in Landsberg, West Germany, they clung to dreams of marriage.
Within weeks of Johnny's arrival home in 1954, they married, moved
to Memphis, and began learning the dance of middle-class family
life. Rosanne was their first child, born May 24, 1955. Less than a
year later, national fame rose around Johnny and dissolved Vivian's
dream of a conventional marriage. Her parochial childhood had prepared her for little beyond making a home for a husband and children, and it certainly had not prepared her for the storms of Johnny's
addictions and the demands of a show business life.

Rosanne long ago accepted that her father was better suited to
June, the twice-married mother of two daughters who enlivened her
father's shows with comic seductiveness and impish duet parts. The
simple fact that June knew the road, knew the Grand Ole Opry,
knew the recording world made her a better fit, and it helped, she
says, that June pricked in Johnny the same impulse toward the coun-

try music tradition that in 1973 inspired him to write the list. "In the beginning," says Rosanne, "it was probably three-quarters of the attraction. This was a woman he'd heard on the radio, and she represented this body of music that was essential. She was another artist. She got it. She had the same kind of respect and passion and love for this music."

Unfortunately, Johnny's drift toward June ruptured Rosanne's childhood. His absences and woozy reappearances at home were bad enough, but Vivian was crashing. In Rosanne's young eyes, her mother became irrational.

"I became an adult at about the age of six. And I took care of my younger sisters in a lot of ways. It's not that my mother wasn't there with dinner on the table, our [school] uniforms were pressed and everything, but emotionally she was a disaster. I mean, I came home every day wondering if my mother was going to be alive. Walk into the house with this unbelievable anxiety in my stomach, and if I saw that there were paper runners on the carpet, that she had had the carpets cleaned, I thought, 'Okay, the carpets are cleaned, the dry cleaning has been delivered, then that means that she thinks she's going to live a while longer. Or else why would she clean the carpets.' So I became the most responsible eight-year-old in the universe.

"She was overwhelmed by her feelings. Her feelings were very primitive, in a way. She made decisions that should have been made out of rational thought out of emotional feeling. She chose a lawyer because he was nice. She [later] chose the person to cowrite her book [*I Walked the Line*, 2007] because she was deferential. You know what I mean? All of these kind of feeling-based decisions. I am a very rational person, and all of this overwhelming feeling was just too much for me. And I lived in my mind and in my ideas, and I learned a lot of very defensive and self-protective ways of living in my house because it was like living in an emergency room."

Vivian and Johnny.

The revelations that Rosanne offers about her mom startle me.
I had always assumed that Rosanne and her sisters weathered childhood without their father because Vivian had been the rock. I knew
that as a child Vivian had had to step into the void left by her al-
coholic mother in order to help keep her household afloat, and so
it followed that she knew how to negotiate around a dysfunctional
family member. But, according to Rosanne, her mother's childhood
offered no preparation for dealing with the Johnny Cash problem.

"My mother was emotionally crippled by her own childhood and
so was not prepared to deal with a husband who was constantly

traveling and a drug addict. I mean, she had absolutely no resources to deal with that. So all the most primitive responses came up, and they were awful. She was debilitated, she was enraged, she was desperate, she was suicidal. I mean, she told this story many, many times that when they finally split, I guess I was about ten or eleven, that she was just so depressed, and a family doctor who was a family friend, said to her, 'Vivian, if you don't get yourself together, then June will be raising your daughters.' And she said that was a turning point for her. But she never got over the bitterness, ever. It's a cautionary tale for me."

Vivian's anger repelled Rosanne, and when it began to mingle with the searching and rebelliousness of her teenage years, living at home in California became untenable. "I left home the day after I graduated from high school, and it really hurt my mother, because I just left. There was no planning, there was no discussion, I just left. My dad came to my high school graduation. Next day I left with him—bye. And it hurt her for years. A few years later I realized how ungracious that was of me and how cruel. And when I was about twenty-one, twenty-two, I wrote her a letter. I said, 'Mom, I realize I never told you I was leaving home in a way that was respectful, so I just want to tell you, I'm leaving home.' But I'd been gone for four years by then. . . . She had a lot of resentment about that. But my mother didn't really understand me. I know she loved me, but she didn't really get me. And I confused her, I scared her. I really see now that I was difficult for her. She really tried, but I think I just scared her."

So, I ask, it boiled down to her stubborn independence? Her mother couldn't understand that?

"Well, how could she not understand stubborn independence?" she exclaims. "She had it in spades. But I guess she didn't understand my particular brand of it. Because she went from her parents' house to her husband's house. A very traditional, strict Catholic girl upbringing. I remember there was this novel called *A Woman of Independent Means* [1978]. . . . I was reading it, and it was a period piece in an epistolary style, and my mother saw the book, and she picked up the book, and she said, 'You need to be more independent? Why are you reading this?'"

While Rosanne negotiated her California childhood, her father was closing in on June Carter. By 1967, he was pleading with her to marry him, although Vivian had not yet granted him a divorce. In response, June was demanding that he clean up his drug and alcohol problems and arrange for her to spend some real time with his daughters. In the rapid, irrational plate tectonics of the Cash-Carter world, June seemed to be sincerely reaching out to Rosanne and her sisters. Of course, Rosanne had no way of knowing that, but her feelings toward June weren't that unpleasant to begin with, despite June's part in her parents' estrangement.

I ask her when June first came into her view. "I remember the Hollywood Bowl show [in 1963] clearly. She did that little bit where she kicked her shoe off. She did this little bit where she had on this beautiful dress, this knee-length, kind of chic dress. And then she would hike it up a little bit, and there would be bloomers underneath. So it was a bit into the show where she'd be kicking and her shoe would go flying. And there is this pool in front of the stage at the Hollywood Bowl, and the shoe went into the pool, so she couldn't retrieve it. So at the age of [eight] that was a powerful memory to me."

And when did she figure out that June was romantically linked to her father? "I don't know that there was a moment," she replies. "There was a dawning awareness that they were together. And that my mom and dad weren't. But it wasn't a devastating thing. It seemed natural to me. I think even then I thought, 'Well, Dad and June are just better suited to each other. They live the same life.'"

"So even in childhood," I venture, "you could accept or see past whatever feelings of loss . . . "

"Well, feelings of loss preceded that," she interjects. "He went on the road when I was six, and a drug addict returned home. That was the loss. The loss was not my parents' breakup. It was his addiction."

"So you let go before your mother let go," I say.

"Absolutely, absolutely. And I remember thinking clearly, when they said they were divorcing, I remember feeling this relief, like maybe both of them will be happy now. That is pretty remarkable for a twelve-year-old to consciously think that, but I did."

It had always seemed ironic to me that Rosanne left her mother in 1973 to live in Nashville with her father and June, whom I thought would have been targets of a two-pronged resentment. But the resentment ran in the opposite direction, back to her mother. "It's not that my dad was that rational either, but at least he didn't make people pay for it, at least not directly."

So, like many eighteen-year-olds, she left home. "It's like, 'I need to find out what I want to do in this world, and I'm not going to find it here.' I don't think I had the cognizance to think, 'Oh, I need to go where I'm accepted.' I was more about adventure and finding myself and spending some time with my dad."

Indeed, she says she journeyed to Nashville hoping her father would give her the kind of carefree childhood she had missed. And he delivered. "It was fantastic. I got a lot of attention from him. He showered gifts on me, took me everywhere. Called me 'princess,' and literally, he called me 'princess' until he died." Her father took her berry picking, churned ice cream with her, let her sing on his records, bought her candy, and invited her to join his road show.

And he disciplined her, she says.

"Rosey [June's daughter] and I would take his car out, this kind of vintage beauty of a car he had. We took it out and got drunk in it, and somebody puked in it, and we brought it back at two in the morning, and Rosey and I are stumbling in and go, 'Okay, we have to get up at six o'clock and go take the car to a car wash before he knows. Well, of course, we sleep until nine. Dad's up at six. He's been out to the car, he's seen what happened, he took the car to a car wash, he came back, he didn't speak to us all day except to say, 'We're going to the farm.' He put us in the car. He's still not saying a word to us, we are absolutely shaking with fear. He pulls into the ice cream shop at Hendersonville, buys us an ice cream, still doesn't say a word, until we get to the farm, two hours later. He's not speaking to us. We are frozen in fear. And we get out, and he sits down on the front steps of the house and just pats the steps beside him for us to come sit by him. We sit down, and he said, 'You could go on the road with me and make a lot of money and see the world, or you could stay home and do drugs.' I'm crying, and go, 'I want to go on the road and make a lot of money and see the world.' And Rosey doesn't answer. Rosey has to think about it. I think she might have said, 'I believe I'll stay home.' But he was great in that way: he wouldn't lose his temper or yell at you or anything, but he could scare you."

It was the time of their reacquaintance.

But it was also her introduction to the Carter Family, the beginning of a relationship that she believes licensed her to sing "Bury Me Under the Weeping Willow Tree" on *The List*. "I had as much love and respect for the music as any of their blood relatives, and June . . . from the first time she took me to Virginia, I was nineteen years old, they were all joking that I was going to marry one of the cousins and end up on the mountain. She'd take me in to her relatives, and they'd say, 'Honey, let me get you a biscuit. You're looking peaked. Let me get you some ham.' And I loved them, I loved the family, I loved the music. I had tremendous respect for it. I didn't have to rebel against the Carter Family music, you know?"

And June, who was raising her toddler John Carter and trying to rein in daughters Rosey and Carlene, proved to be Rosanne's unexpected companion. "She claimed me for her own. She did. She told me she felt like I was her daughter. I was very close to her. She taught me a lot. We were flying first-class to Europe, and I was sitting next to June, and this flight attendant brought this cart by with caviar. This was in the days when they actually fed you on airplanes. And I turned up my nose at the caviar, and June took some, and she just kind of looked at me very sweetly and she said, 'You're the type of woman who would love caviar.' And it was so forceful the way she said it, just this kind of understanding of me before I could understand myself. So I said, 'I'll have some.' And of course, I did. . . . That's kind of emblematic of a thousand ways she initiated me, to talk to me about men and clothing and social niceties and flowers and behavior. She was very retro in the way she saw a woman's role with men, and at the same time she lived her life exactly as she wanted.

"She was crazy like a fox in some ways. That kind of frivolous exterior masked a really incisive person who . . . I don't want to use the word 'manipulative' . . . but she would and did manipulate her environment to serve her in many, many ways. But she was also . . . she just thought differently than anyone, and as she got older the kind of gaps in her coherence got larger, and it was charming. In some ways it was very charming, but in other ways she was just not on the planet.

"The way she saw family was really fascinating. I remember once they were on the road, they were playing up in the Catskills, and I was already in New York, and I went up to see them, and I took [daughter] Carrie, Carrie was about three years old, and she let Carrie sleep with her. Carrie was three. And she also would lay on the floor and let Carrie brush her hair out in huge wings around her,

Johnny and June on stage.

like a huge arc, you know how long her hair was. She was a sixty-five-year-old woman, and she would lay flat on the floor for an hour and let Carrie brush her hair out in a circle! And then she would mimic what Carrie did, and it was adorably cute. It was more just her persona and who she was. That was just unusual. She was an unusual person."

Rosanne arrived in the Cash-Carter world during a time when Johnny and June were projecting to the public an image of familial perfection: home fires burning, church on Sunday, dinners around the kitchen table. Rosanne says she bought into the family fusion of those days, but I observe that in pictures I've seen of her among June's daughters and sisters and nieces and nephews, she seems uneasy.

"I was uncomfortable in my own skin," she protests. "It wasn't anything that they did. I mean, I have this picture of me about nineteen, just long straight hair just kind of looking down, just falling apart internally, and June sitting next to me with her arm around me, really strong, just holding me up. I remember that day so clearly. I was falling apart inside at nineteen . . . , like, 'I don't know what I want to do with my life, and do I ever want to get married, and will I ever find the right man, and what am I going to be.' And it was just overwhelming, and June was a rock. In many ways, she offered more support to me around that stuff than my dad did."

"Did she mother you in a way that your own mother couldn't?" I ask.

"She did, because number one she didn't have any of the natural tension that biological mothers and daughters have. So she was free of that. So she didn't have the anxiety about me, about what I was going to do, that my own mother did. My own mother had a lot of anxiety about me. And June was just accepting, and June had been in this business for her whole life, so she didn't have any anxiety about that either. Like, 'Well, if you [become an entertainer] that's great.' She just lived very large, and she wasn't made nervous by other people who lived large. And so she thought that there was a world of possibilities that could all be great. My own mother thought there was a world of possibilities, most of which would be dangerous. So I got something from [June]. There was some permission that I didn't get [earlier].

"She also understood artists, and it didn't frighten her. She knew that artists have to push boundaries and go to extremes sometimes, and go to really dark places, and that they can come back. She was fine with all that."

While June schooled Rosanne in the prerogatives of art and stardom, June's sister Helen, the eldest of Mother Maybelle's three

daughters, schooled Rosanne in music. "It was a powerful reintro-
duction to country music, because the two and a half years I was
on the road with my dad after high school and sitting in the dressing
room with Helen and Maybelle and Anita too—Anita was drifting
a lot—Helen in particular was completely focused on teaching me
these songs. That's when I learned to play guitar, eighteen, nineteen
years old, by learning 'Banks of the Ohio' and 'Black Jack David,'
'Merry Golden Tree,' those kinds of things. Around that same time
Dad made the list for me. And that was one part of it. But it was
abstract in the beginning. What was not abstract was Helen teaching me to play 'Banks of the Ohio.' And me going, 'Wow, the last
thing I listened to was Buffalo Springfield, the last thing I remember
before learning "Banks of the Ohio."'" It was powerful, and then this
whole lexicon opened up, and it made a huge impact on me.

"Dad would be onstage. So we would have an hour and a half or
whatever to sit there before we all would go out for 'Will the Circle
Be Unbroken.' So I would sit with Helen, and Carl [Perkins] too
actually, but Carl would have his guitar, and he'd be riffing and playing other stuff. But Helen and Maybelle would show me a couple
of things. Anita would show me a couple of things, [but] she'd drift
in and out. But Helen was very focused. I'd say, 'But how do you
do this?' and then, 'Where does it go?' and 'How do you make the
G chord?' and 'How do you get quickly from the G to the C?' And
she was very, very patient. Carl would show me a couple of things,
but like I said, he'd get distracted easily. And the way I learned to
play guitar is to learn all of these three-chord songs. And there was
plenitude.

"I loved Helen so much. I just adored her. She was like a fragile
little bird when I first really got to know her. Of course, I'd known
her from the time I was twelve, but when I first really got to know
her, she had just lost her son. Kenny [Jones] had just died [in a car

Helen, Mother Maybelle, and June at Sunset Park in Pennsylvania, 1962.

accident], and she was incredibly nervous, and she was on the verge of a little bit of a breakdown all the time. And she had to take things to calm her nerves, and she was a little bit of a mess, except when she was onstage. Then she was utterly focused, completely proficient in what she was doing. And she was playing guitar. If I remember correctly, she and Maybelle would play guitar. She would play guitar, and Maybelle would play autoharp. I don't think June and Anita ever played an instrument. June may have played auto-harp a couple of times. But anyway, Helen was the rhythm, and she had to hold it together. So everything she found hard to hold together in her private life, she was a master at onstage. And I have to think it gave her some pleasure to teach me all these songs."

CHAPTER 7

Miss the Mississippi and You

Mid-February. The familiar cold wind howls down Sixth Avenue, against traffic. Men in heavy canvas jackets line up outside a construction site in hopes of work, while customers gather across the street in front of the large home electronics store waiting for the doors to open. A mother whose displeasure rings from two storefronts away walks abreast of her daughter who wears a purple wig. "Don't answer me with that whiney voice, Brianna," the mother spits. "It's your fault. I asked you to do something. . . ." The admonishment fades out of earshot, so I assume she finishes with " . . . and you ignored me," which is likely because that is what Brianna is trying to do.

Except for the mother-daughter spat, quiet blankets this Chelsea morning. The puppies in the doggie hotel yelp and yip and roll over each other, while a few blocks away neighbors cheerfully lug boxes of clothing and other donations into the local Salvation Army store.

This afternoon Rosanne is due at the studio to record vocals for three songs: "Miss the Mississippi and You," "Satisfied Mind," and "Sea of Heartbreak." And then she is to rush to an evening fundraiser for her son's school, where she is supposed to perform a few songs and sit in front of the audience for an interview with a *New Yorker* writer who is also a parent. This morning she is sitting for an interview with me.

Her foot has improved, so she glides as she leads me into the kitchen, where her father's "One Piece at a Time," about stealing auto parts, is blaring on the radio. The WNYC hosts are discussing the sickly auto industry. Rosanne smiles, and then tells me before we start that she'll need to save a few minutes to find the lyrics for "Miss the Mississippi" on the web. So we get started immediately. Well, almost immediately. Very few starts are immediate with Rosanne. First she runs upstairs to fetch socks and shoes and brush makeup on her face. When she sits down at the kitchen table and begins to slide her socks onto her bare feet, I ask her about Europe. Next week she begins a weeklong tour of Switzerland and Germany with a television appearance in Scotland. Our talk soon turns to children and leaving them behind for work.

Ironically, her father had cautioned her to take care of her family before serving the call of career. "That weighed heavily on him," she says.

"I didn't need that warning. I had such a hyperreactive alarm system about being away from my kids too much. I kind of became famous in Nashville for not touring. Even as much as I toured, which was nothing compared to my contemporaries, I still feel guilty about how much I was away. By the time of *Interiors*, I probably did forty dates or fifty dates in back of that record, but spread out. That was a lot for me then. . . . I don't have regrets about that at all. There's not been one day when I say, 'I wish I would have gone out more.' No. It probably took me longer to find my place onstage, just that chemical place, or alchemical place. But I appreciate it more. I'm not burned out at fifty-three. I still really appreciate it and love it.

"It's interesting how some fans perceive that. I've gotten angry e-mails and angry letters from people who say, 'I guess you'll just never come to Pocatello. I guess we don't rate on your radar.' I say, 'Ma'am, there's a lot of places I haven't been.'"

Back to children, she confesses to feeling anxiety about leaving son Jake for nine days to make her dates in Europe even though big sister Carrie and John will be returning home before the final leg of her journey, a stop in Scotland. "In one way, it's a little silly because Jake is going to camp for three weeks this summer, so it's not like he's not able to do this, but I still suffer the whole time. I'll never forget when he was four, I went to Japan for five days. Japan for five days is tough, but I didn't want to stay longer because he was little. And John stayed home. And John told me that the night I left, he was putting him to bed and he said, 'Dad, I'm thinking of ways to make Mom come home.' So I think of that all the time. 'I'm thinking of ways to make Mom come home.' He went to camp for ten days last summer, and I said, 'Did you miss us?' And he said, 'To tell you the truth, sometimes I forgot I had parents.' So I guess we've done an okay job with him.

"I was talking to somebody the other night who's on the road a lot. He's a finance guy, and he was thinking about being away from his kids, but then he thought about the old days when whaling captains would go off for two and a half years, wouldn't see their kids. He said, 'So I kind of slap myself around and go, "Get over it. You're gone for five days."'"

As Rosanne suggests, her reluctance to tour remains one of the major themes of her long career in music. In fact, if you take the time to page through the hundreds of articles written about her over the past thirty years, you'll find that they follow a formula: her father, her introspective lyrics, and—as regular as a daily train—her unwillingness to tour.

Rosanne with (l to r) Loretta Lynn, Reba McEntire, and Holly Dunn in 1987.

- "I'm reluctant about getting caught up in the mechanism," she told the *Orlando Sentinel* in 1986. "There's a certain myth of stardom and a certain formula of stardom I don't buy. I really believe in an individual approach to life, so I just follow my instincts, and my instincts tell me it's not good to be away from small children for lengthy tours. My dad wasn't around too much when I was a kid, and I just don't want to do that to my kids. So I don't."

- "I just don't enjoy touring that much," she admitted to the *Boston Globe* one year later. "My tours have been short and sporadic. It's just not something I wanted to commit to. It's not a formula I felt I had to follow."

- "Well, you know, there's a formula in Nashville about how you should make records, how you should relate to your audience, how much you should tour," she reiterated to Alanna Nash in the early 1980s. "The whole thing is a package deal.

They might as well turn it into a handbook and give it to you as you enter the business. And I *just don't buy it*! I don't buy it at all! I think there's an individual way to approach life and success. . . . But I don't think that I have to tour to sell records. I just don't. Maybe I'd be selling five times as many if I did tour, but I don't know that, so it doesn't irk me."

In fact, one can also see in those articles that in and around various album release dates over the years she could be counted on to be in a state of expectant motherhood. Hard to mount a tour with a child in the womb. And hard to gather and maintain an audience from the foot of a baby's crib.

Her manager, Danny Kahn, accepts and understands Rosanne's limited touring, acknowledging, however, that she could cultivate larger audiences and tally up bigger record sales if she hit the road more often. He's philosophical about his artist: "She does what she needs to do and sometimes even a little bit more. Touring—it's a long conversation—but it's a relative thing based on how an artist perceives her own life. There are many artists that live for the stage and performing and that audience feedback and have given everything over to that life on the road, even raising families on the road or not. While other artists—and I have to say Rosanne would be one of those other artists—try to find a way to do it to satisfy both obligations and enjoyment of performing in balance with the rest of private and professional life that doesn't involve touring. For her, the rest of that life is pretty dense and involved, so it's quite easy for her to be very busy but not tour nearly as much as most artists. That's the way we do it. We try to be creative and strategic. Nothing's etched in stone: there may still be a time in her life when she'll get to it a little bit more because something in her head wants her to."

There may have been a time when Kahn saw that the link between touring and records sales was stronger and therefore Rosanne's refusal to mortgage herself to the road was more damaging to her record sales, but he's not so sure anymore. "The record business is going through so much turmoil and transition that it's hard to say what does what. Everything in the news today is how the Grammy telecast had less of an influence on the sales of the Grammy winners and the telecast performers than before. There are definite patterns of artists both young and older who do incredibly well touring and selling tickets for live performances, and very few records are sold. So in some ways the two industries are almost separate from each other more than they've ever been. Performing is its own business, and selling records is another business. And some artists are even willing to give away records because most of their business and moneymaking operation is on the live circuit. So these challenges are greatest for artists like Rosanne and managers like me; we're more used to doing it a particular way, and the new way isn't at all obvious to us, and even if it were, we may not be able to plug into it because of who the audience is. But clearly Rosanne is somewhere in the midst of an incredible career and is a well-known artist with years of experience. She has an advantage of not just starting out. There are people who know her everywhere, and as long as she's good, there will be people coming to see her. Not to say that she's failing or our business is failing; there are just wild challenges compared to what it used to be."

At the big kitchen table with Rosanne, I tell her that many seem to admire her for making choices with Jake and her daughters in mind, and whether it does any good in the end, it seems like the right thing to do. "It does to me," she replies.

It's another Gansevoort day, so I collect my things while Rosanne dashes upstairs to search for the "Miss the Mississippi" lyrics. I climb to the second floor moments later to find her at the computer, listening to the original Jimmie Rodgers recording and scanning the lyrics from Bob Dylan's website. Rosanne sings along. In a weird way, I feel like I'm witnessing a humming line in the American musical tradition: a granddaughter of country music connecting with *the* grandfather.

Back downstairs, Rosanne throws on a long black winter coat, while she looks for laundry to take to the dry cleaners and complains about missing her iPhone, which daughter Carrie recently put down on a shelf in Barney's department store and forgot to pick up. What will the breaks at the studio be like today without the iPhone? She's also scratching her head over an automated message that has been left on another cell phone lying around the house. It says that there's been an event at Jake's school and that school officials are seeing to it. She assumes that the electricity is out or a water main has burst, but Rosanne dials the school to find out more. But she gets the same vague story. The secretary assures her that if there's more news to report, she will call. Rosanne gives her John's cell phone number, and we head downtown.

On Gansevoort Street, John puts the band through drills. It's the first time in the life of *The List* that he and Rosanne have worked with the band. Up to this point, she has sung to John's instrumental tracks, with drummers Joe Bonadio and Shawn Pelton chiming in only on a few sessions. Today, a bass player who resembles Trey Anastasio of Phish and an organist who plays a Leslie-brand unit and tours with Steely Dan join Joe on drums and John on guitar. A serious tone, far more serious than the demo sessions, colors the date. Rick DePofi has brought in an assistant named Adam to fetch cords and order lunch; the young fellow darts around the studio trying to anticipate needs and respond to Rick's barked orders. He has strapped a massaging cushion to a chair for Rosanne, and when recording begins he will drape a blanket over the door, which is wedged open by a cord that runs from the organ to its gently humming speaker outside the room. In a more hedonistic era, when record company budgets knew no limits, there might have been an elaborate food spread, all kinds of drinks, and an assortment of other goodies. Instead, lunch will be delivered in paper bags, and only a belt of whiskey from the kitchen will ease the mind.

As always, John's energy dominates the room. Even Rosanne—the star—shrinks in comparison. She enters the studio almost unnoticed and quietly greets the assembled. All eyes rest on John. He stands up and, like a boy who's just hooked his first fish, tells Rosanne that he's been wanting to bring the organist to one of her sessions ever since seeing him perform on stage three years before. She seems ready to go along with John's instincts. Those instincts drive this process, like when something's not sitting right about the last four bars of "Miss the Mississippi." He doesn't say specifically and perhaps can't say specifically, but he asks to run through those bars one more time. From his folding metal chair set on a Persian rug, he will say "one more time," but as with Rosanne's vocal track sessions earlier in the winter, there's never just one more. He asks in a casual tone and attempts to tweak his band's performances with a vague yet apparently effective glossary: "that's too *churchy*," "too *loungey*," "*jazzy*," "a little *nice*," "could be a little *trashier*." John levels criticism that is restrained, yet unsweetened. And the artists accept it.

Producer Brian Wilson has talked about hearing the music in his head, and I think John may know what the famed Beach Boy means. He has a notion of what he wants to hear from the very beginning and coaches his musicians along until they get it. As he deals with those last four bars later in the session, he will ask the organist to perform various fills that will give him options. He asks him to play on the beat, to play behind the beat, to do a chord-based fill and then to do a fill that conjures the melody. However, none of them pleases him. Finally, John drops it, telling the organist that he will assemble a fill from those takes that will make him, the organist, look good. So the listener will get a composite organ solo—if it makes the album—one that never existed in an organic form yet did exist as music in John's head.

He seems somewhat agitated today. Perhaps because the stakes are so high: the performances recorded today will be on the finished tracks. Or perhaps he's put off because I am there to observe, threatening to demystify the music-making process. Fair enough. I acutely feel that I'm intruding when I approach him to ask about his timeline. Will the record label take these tracks and work with them?

"What?" he demands, squinting his eyes as he looks at me. "Wha . . . I don't understand what you're saying."

I re-state my question, re-arranging a few words in hopes of making myself clear.

"You don't understand what's going on here, do you? We don't change the music when it leaves here."

I feel the blood of embarrassment crawl up my neck, but I remain collected enough to remind him that during the session that Bestor Cram shot earlier in the month, Mahattan's Mike Bailey injected a suggestion or two. "He won't do it again when he receives the tracks?" I ask.

"Well," says John, his tension subsiding a little. "We let them think they have a say."

Although Jerry Lee Lewis, Emmylou Harris and other great artists have recorded composer William Halley's "Miss the Mississippi and You" over the years, it's Jimmie Rodgers' seminal version recorded in 1932 in New York City, less than two miles away from Gansevoort Street, that rings in Rosanne's ears as she navigates the baffles and the studio slash covering the floor on the way to the recording booth.

As she settles in the booth, John visits the rhythm he will create on his guitar and shouts over to his wife, making sure that she has adequate volume in her headphones. "Let's go," he orders. "And a one and a two and a three . . . " The band strikes up a minstrel shuffle that recalls a congregation of American musicians: Gene Austin, Emmett Miller, Lonnie Johnson, and even Bob Dylan when he recorded "Bye and Bye" and "Po' Boy" for 2001's *Love and Theft*. I can almost see the Singing Brakeman nestle against the wall and, with a pleased grin on his face, light a cigarette, or Larry Campbell, his long hair hanging down around his face, bearing down on his guitar, eyes closed, down in the groove.

I'm getting tired of these big city lights / Tired of the glamour and tired of the sights . . .

In two takes, Rosanne and the band create a "Miss the Mississippi and You" that satisfies John.

The next words out of John's mouth would probably be, "Let's try 'Satisfied Mind,'" but his cell phone vibrates, buzzing on the metal music stand where he has laid it.

John picks up cautiously. It's his son's school, and judging from John's impatient reaction, it seems to be as vague as it was with Rosanne. "What happened?" he demands. Silence. And then John gasps. Rosanne tentatively steps from the sound booth in the direction of her husband. "We'll be right there," he says and sets down the phone.

A schoolmate of Jake's has passed away.

Rosanne rushes to collect her things.

The moment brings me back to my childhood when two fellow students died in my school. Even now when a student in the college where I teach dies, it's always met with palpable sorrow and unpredictable grieving. John and Rick recalls deaths of students during their school days and how they processed those experiences.

I wonder how Jake is taking it.

Rosanne speeds away in a taxi to find out.

Obviously, the school cancels the evening fund-raiser. And John leads the band through two more songs before calling it a day.

A few weeks later, Rosanne tells me about collecting Jake from school. He was not taking the situation well.

He was pale and shaking. She tried to engage him, but he had little to say while waiting to see a school psychologists. "[The counseling] was really beneficial to children who are naturally outgoing and would talk about it. It didn't do so much for my child who was not speaking out and not expressive of his feelings, but he did get to observe his friends talking about it which I think was just as helpful to him. His friends would express feelings for him. One boy said, 'I cried and I was scared . . . ,' all the same that Jake feels, but it's just somebody else saying it for him."

Looking out on to Gansevoort Street.

"I found out a lot about Jake in this whole process. I thought, 'Oh my God he needs to talk about it, I'm so worried he's not talking about it and he's not expressing these feelings about it.' And finally I realized, 'Well, *my* way of doing things is to talk about it and actually talk about it over and over, to reduce the trauma.' I just learned he's a completely different person, if I didn't know it before. And the way he dealt with it, I actually had a tremendous amount of respect for him and still do. It's actually changed my thinking about him and who he is. It's not just his stoicism, although he is a very stoic child, but he keeps his own counsel and his inner life is private to him and he has a resiliency. I was so afraid he's going to fall apart—'what's going to happen to him?—and he did kind of fall apart in his own way for a few days. He didn't eat, and I could tell he was anxious and a bit depressed, but then he managed his feelings and after two weeks he's back to his normal self. I think it's definitely going to come back on him, but I have full confidence that he is going to know how to deal with that too. I mean the best you can do is just reflect back to them what they need and be there and hold the space and that's all I tried to do. This was a shock in so many ways and so I thought about it and I said, 'You know, when I was in sixth grade somebody in high school died and I was really scared, were you really scared?' Then he opened up a little bit. He said, 'Yes, I was really scared.'"

All of this upheaval leaves the European tour in question. Everything in Switzerland, Germany, and Scotland is booked, but in the days immediately after the news spread around the school, Jake is refusing food and complaining of an upset stomach. Rosanne thinks about scotching the tour. "I've done that twice in my life where I cancelled a tour, and it's not pretty," she says. "They got litigious on me." So, she and John invite him to come along. "Is there anything fun to do in Europe?" Jake asks. But before Rosanne can answer, he tells her he'd rather stay home with sister Carrie and his toys.

As Jake's appetite returns and his shaking disappears and he returns to his routine, she and John decide that they will go and that John will come home five days into the travels, after the second of three shows in Germany. A cell phone proves to be another remedy. Jake has been lobbying for one, so in light of the circumstances, Rosanne concedes. "I didn't frame it that I'm buying it because this happened. . . . He had been asking for one for a while so I thought, 'Okay. This is perfect.' And it actually did calm him down."

Throughout the tour, Rosanne will text and call Jake and Carrie often. When she returns, she will find Jake playing with his toy soldiers.

CHAPTER 8

Silver Wings

Friday, February 27. I am on board a British Airways flight to London at 6:30 PM, walking through first class and business class, rolling my eyes as I see passengers already nuzzled into their plush seats, flutes of champagne and velvet dark juices on their trays. As if I am being punished for leaving my children for a week, I find myself in steerage seated amid a group of high school students who munch on fruit chews, rub their noses, and fiddle with their MP3 players. I'm somewhat relieved when I see one or two pull out Sudoku puzzles and sports magazines. Perhaps it is an intellectual crowd.

The passenger in front of me reclines his chair deep into my knees, and I picture Rosanne cruising across the Atlantic in first class. Indeed, Rosanne left Thursday evening, loading onto a Continental flight in Newark with John and Danny. They were to meet the band in Zurich and play on the evening of their arrival, which sounds impossible to me, but Rosanne has packed her engagements into as few days as possible in order to get back to Jake as soon as she can. As it is, John will leave after their third show—in Cologne—to fly back home. So, by this time next week, Rosanne will have played five concerts and be in the midst of taping a television show in Scotland for the BBC. I guess she deserves that first-class seat.

From my seat, I can hear the boys conversing about their music, which amounts to another lesson in the challenges facing the recording industry. "What are you listening to, Ted?" one of the mop-topped kids calls from across a row of seats. "Just some music from video games," he replies. Now that one was new on me. Evidently—and I'm showing my age, I guess—Ted has ripped music from his Grand Theft Auto. Is that legal? Will Interpol be waiting for him when he steps off the plane in London? One of Ted's friends echoes my questions, showing surprising concern about the law. Ted admits—with a healthy amount of swagger in his cracking voice—that he's stockpiled twenty-one songs the way Jesse James might have done it were he galloping through the Internet today. The boys around Ted nod in unison, appreciating that their friend has found another way to circumnavigate the recording industry—another way, to my way of thinking, not to buy a Rosanne Cash album.

Why would he be interested in a Rosanne Cash album, you ask? Well, I was when I was Ted's age. *King's Record Shop.* I owned it in its totality, with the factory-pressed vinyl disc *and* original cardboard sleeve.

I've thought about the mingling of music and video games before. After a Gansevoort date, while waiting for a sandwich, Rosanne bemoaned a new device by Microsoft called Songsmith. "It lets you write a song, even if you know nothing about music," she complained, sipping a stemless glass of wine. "This is what music is coming to." Taking up the new technology theme, I suggest to both her and John that the day may be coming when she will have to embed her music in a video game. She chuckles as if to dismiss the notion. John seems intrigued. But we change the topic.

I arrive in Zurich via London in the bright early afternoon. Trams hum as they snake down narrow streets, muted from time to time by the thumpy sound of pigeons taking flight. A few hearty souls sip coffee at sidewalk cafés, while parents and children clutching snowboards and skis make their way to buses and trains that will take them to the numerous slopes that circle the city. Neat clusters of homes climb the hills that surround the town, not unlike the enclaves one sees above Hollywood or Seattle. And Zurich is clean—perhaps not as clean as Rosanne observed when she wrote once that the nation "routinely vacuums its sidewalks," but nonetheless amazingly pristine compared to gritty New York. It's so neat that I'm amazed to observe a homeless man in a worn cap and holey sweater pluck a paper cup from a trash can, gulp down the remaining drink, and then drop it into the next can he passes.

Somewhere in town Rosanne, John, and Danny—clutching their own cups of coffee—explore the shore of Lake Zurich, probably reviewing last night's show as they walk. I'll learn later that Rosanne and the musicians stumbled more times than any of them would have liked and that massive clouds of cigarette smoke irritated Rosanne's throat. She's obviously forgotten what bars and restaurants were like in pre–smoking law New York. As for the missteps, perhaps they could have been avoided had the troupe rehearsed.

They get another chance tonight.

Tonight my tram drops me at its last stop on a line that stretches from downtown to a high peak on the southwestern edge of the city. I'm steps from the Albisgüetli, a huge restaurant and convention hall that for tonight has been transformed into Europe's largest barn dance. Darkness swallows the last hint of afternoon, revealing strings of light that run along the turreted roof. A waxing moon appears with a thousand twinkling stars. Countless church steeples come into view in the valley bathed in spotlights.

Under a neon cowboy hat, a line of Swiss dressed in tassels, black cowboy hats, and bolero ties forms. Do they think it's a Clint Black concert? Harley-Davidson and Chevrolet are major sponsors of the

Rosanne and John in Zurich.

show, so their banners are everywhere. The line outside wanders by a fleet of new Chevy models, and I hope—mindful of the precarious state of General Motors in 2009—that the promoter has gotten his sponsorship money in advance. In minutes, more than a thousand people join the line. Their numbers will swell to more than two thousand, each of whom is paying fifty-five Swiss francs for admission and more for their beer and food.

Rosanne confesses embarrassment that I'm seeing her play Europe's take on a hoedown. "It's so fetishized," she says of the Swiss embrace of country music. "There are all of these stands for cowboy hats and belts and whatever, all this stuff that's kind of country, actually country *and* western, big emphasis on the western part. So it's a little bit like a Star Trek convention. A lot of Trekkies out there. I didn't really get it the first time I went, so I wore a really nice lace blouse and black pants, and I show up and I could tell it was just utterly disappointing, so [this time] I am wearing my Manuel jacket with embroidery designs.

"It's got to be more heavily the hits and more country. . . . I know I have to tailor the show for this. Like I said, the first time I did it I didn't really get it, and there was a little bit of a disconnect between me and them. So I get it this time. I get what they want, and they are paying me well, so I am going to do what I can do. I'll just make sure I do some of the new stuff from *The List*, which would be really good, really appropriate. Also some big hits, 'Runaway Train' and that kind of stuff."

Inside Albisgüetli, the suede leather vests and bandannas find their places at long tables or crowd around the bar in the back. Waiters and waitresses carry plates of food that would make any American proud: chili, steak, and a hamburger for two that looks like a three-layer chocolate cake. It's amusing to hear the Swiss pronounce "fajitas," but their orders are clear, and the fajitas emerge from the kitchen in rapid succession. Bottles of Miller Genuine Draft pop at the bar as well as bottles of Coke—made with sugar, not corn syrup, the way it was meant to be. But both of these iconic American beverages are dwarfed by the huge bottles of Bavarian beer that make a thud when their caps are pried off.

Never mind that at this very moment the Obama administration is trying to shake loose money from secretive Swiss banks that shield tax dollars due the U.S. government—America rules this venue. Huge U.S. flags billow on the ceiling, and red-white-and-blue bunting festoons the balconies. I can't remember the last time I saw an American flag unfurled in Europe that was not in flames. It feels good actually.

So in light of the abundant American regalia and the name on the marquee, I'm surprised there's not more Johnny Cash iconography in the house tonight. A few records and DVDs by the Man in Black sit in a makeshift music store, but they equal the number of Rosanne Cash records. I expect to see her father's name on belt buckles, bandannas, and beer mugs, but I only see him once, on a belly: a man with a hefty gut squeezes between two tables, showing off on his T-shirt a stunning reproduction of the cover of Cash's first *American Recordings* album.

A decade ago, Rosanne wrote in an article for *New York* magazine that one should never play a country music festival in Switzerland. Fans, she said, "will dress up as cowboys, get inhumanly drunk, and shoot real guns at the ceiling during your performance." This evening she has ignored her own advice, but has found an audience considerably tamer than what she described.

Danny Kahn fetches her from a dressing room behind a door in the corner of the hall and leads her through a maze of tabletops crowded with brown bottles and empty plates to the side of the stage. A boyish master of ceremonies warms the audience in staccato German, before exclaiming a phrase that even I understand: "Rosanne Cash!" The funky first bars of "I'm Movin' On" throb from the stage, communicating that *The List* is very much on her mind and will be tested in Switzerland and on down the European road. Tonight she will add two numbers from the album—"Miss the Mississippi and You" and "Sea of Heartbreak"—and they will prove to be among her most heartfelt offerings.

Rosanne wastes no time reaching out to her country-inclined audience. On the heels of the Hank Snow classic, she treats them to her own country classic: "Seven Year Ache." A crowd migrates to the stage, and chatting diners stop for a moment to consider the music, and the cameras flash to life. Those wielding them dominate the floor in front of Rosanne, elbowing the dancers and the drinkers who have abandoned the bar to see more. Between songs, Rosanne banters, complimenting Lake Zurich and explaining the list that her father gave her in 1973, but the language barrier—despite

Rosanne with John and bassist Jeff Allen.

Rosanne's good-willed German greetings—dampens the exchange. She'll have to rely on the more-than-capable ambassador that is her music.

When the photographers finally scatter, fans and dancers take over the floor, where they will remain for most of the twenty-one-song set. Others ingest their Rosanne from bar stools and up against walls. A group ensconced on a soft leather sofa tell me that Rosanne is "beautiful" and they saw her the last time she performed here. One of the group teaches line dancing and prefers Rosanne's 1980s hits. I suspect that many of his countrymen agree, as a significant swath of them are keeping their distance, figuratively and physically. They refuse to give Rosanne much feedback even as she samples her father's catalog and revisits her own major country hits, like "Blue

Two fans in Zurich.

Moon with Heartache" and "Runaway Train." Instead, they watch stone-faced or hardly break from their conversation while Rosanne churns on. Perhaps they sense her ambivalence toward the date. Indeed, she seems somewhat detached. Although she smiles graciously for the fans and cameras, she most often projects a curious gaze, slightly serious, somewhat playful, but ultimately elusive.

Or perhaps she senses *their* ambivalence. For many of the ticket-holders, this show could be more about the scene than about seeing Rosanne, an opportunity to strut their western feathers amid a flock of peers. A few Europeans I meet in Germany will theorize later in the week that the Swiss lack national character—a result of their long and dearly held neutrality—so they flirt with various foreign identities to compensate. A night at the Albisgüetli becomes a much-craved search for meaning and community.

For a while, I forget that I'm in Zurich. The scene could be a big dance hall in Louisiana Cajun country or the piney woods of East

Texas, places where the patrons take center stage. So many musical events these days focus so intensely on the artist that crowd response seems scripted. Men and women are confined to their seats, all of which face the artist like pews before an altar. Here in Zurich it's not so artist-centric. Clients practice their dance routines, flirt with their barmaids, or preen in their western dress as Rosanne almost becomes backdrop. Tiny dramas unfold everywhere. Off in a corner, a ten-year-old girl gives a young woman line-dancing lessons, a pretty hostess tries without success to lure patrons to a display of Chevrolet automobiles, and a trio of late-middle-aged men try to roust a dozing patron from his spot on a sofa so they can sit together and drink, puff cigars, and guffaw.

Despite last night's wrong turns and the constant smoke that crashes the stage like surf, Rosanne and the band hit all their marks. The band's rhythm—charged by drummer Dave Mattacks, formerly of Fairport Convention, and bass player Jeff Allen—is reliably constant, and Rosanne early on finds her place in it. She takes her acoustic guitar from the stand and joins the band, her rhythm accentuating her mates', the instrument's varnished top flashing in time as it moves in and out of the spotlight's glare. Throughout the night, she flat-out rocks, spinning and strutting and stomping her foot. A sultry siren, she sways and feels the music.

And the Swiss will accept it.

During intermission, John Leventhal, who has been dutifully leading Rosanne and the band, walks to the darkened stage and wanders around it. He seems lost or out of place. Hands in his pockets, he leans over and examines what look to be guitar picks splayed out on top of an amplifier. Over the loudspeaker, a mainstream country song blares, and John is wearing a wrinkled western shirt. A bearded Swiss ambles over to him to fawn over his playing, praise that John accepts but not without obvious discomfort. He greets it with a pained smile.

Onstage when the music begins again, John appears to find a peace. He steps aside for Rosanne, who continues to make her point, balancing her country with the later auteurism that shows up in performances such as "Burn Down This Town" and "God Is in the Roses" from *Black Cadillac*. I wonder what she's thinking as she looks out to see line dancers shuffling with their backs to her and a Harley-Davidson poster staring boldly back at her. Surely she knows that nary a body in the place is contemplating her painfully hewn lyrics. When I ask Danny Kahn how often Rosanne finds herself in a scene so western in the United States, he grins: "Once every three years." At the Albisgüetli, it's as if Rosanne is playing the Reo Palm Isle in Longview, Texas, or the Pepsi Roadhouse outside Pittsburgh, venues that Rosanne would never dream of visiting. But tonight in Zurich, where the mountains and the steeples brush against the sky, she is well outside the intelligentsia's radar. And the money is good.

Back in New York, I had thought that *The List*—once it's released—might have the potential to pull Rosanne back into the country music world, taking her full circle to the 1980s, her golden decade. Indeed, if Manhattan marketed the album as a Nashville homecoming, the country music media might dash to the hook and yank her back into the room with her 1980s competitors, many of whom, like Crystal Gayle, make big money on the casino and fair circuit or, like Reba McEntire, who also came of age in the eighties, remain fixtures of the country music establishment.

Zurich tells me that Rosanne will resist any such temptation. She has no designs on the country music market. The genre gave her a base, as did her name, but she prefers to use it in search of new artistic veins.

If Zurich hadn't told me of Rosanne's resistance to the echoes of her country music past, Danny Kahn would have. He often finds

himself warding off American promoters who want her for their rodeos and jamborees and the reporters who call incessantly to ask about Johnny Cash.

Something of a renaissance man, Kahn follows art and culture like a college football fan and runs an architectural camp for children in New Hampshire. Rosanne, though, receives his most intense focus. They met in 1995 when Rosanne's then-manager, Will Botwin, took a job with Sony. Botwin recommended Kahn, who was just leaving Elektra/Nonesuch Records. "From our first meeting," says Rosanne, "we decided to work together, and it's always been on a handshake—we've never signed a contract with each other.

"We're both mercurial, and we both like the world of ideas, so we get into talking about ideas, concepts, visions, and Danny plays it a little close to the vest, but he was so instrumental in the *Black Cadillac* show. . . . He said, 'Look . . . let's divide up the show, let's make this show something really special, a theatrical kind of show,' so he had the vision for that, which was fantastic. He also has really good instincts about what I shouldn't do. And they invariably match mine."

When I ask her for an example of requests he fends off, Rosanne mentions a recent call from a noted female country singer's manager. "They wanted me to sing on her record, and Danny said, 'Well, what song?' And she said, 'I don't know.' 'Well, is this a featured part, is it a duet?' 'No, we just want her to sing harmony, we don't know which songs.' So he went, 'Well, no.' He has a good sense for respect and quality and dignity. He is also a good business guy. And he doesn't lose it, he's not disrespectful."

A Boston native, Kahn began his life in the music business in the 1970s, when he helped establish a radio station in Madison, Wisconsin, and booked blues bands from nearby Chicago on the side. In the 1980s, he landed an executive position with Elektra/Nonesuch, where his work with the Bulgarian State Female Vocal Choir helped usher in the age of world music and garnered a Grammy Award for the choir. Music fans might also know about his association with rhythm-and-blues journeyman Arthur Alexander, who recorded his great comeback album, *Lonely Just Like Me*, in 1993 under Kahn's sponsorship, only to die before the album's release.

Head shaved close, black-framed glasses perched on his face, and always in dark clothing, Kahn models the urban intellectual, yet he remains knee-deep in the gravel and fire of the music industry. Eminently patient with the conflict and minutiae that crops up on the road, he is the fixer, the money guy, the soother, the caretaker. The manager. And he never fails with perspective, analysis, and good old-fashioned spin for a writer following his client through Switzerland, Germany, and Scotland.

CHAPTER 9

Five Hundred Miles Away

The Zurich sunshine that greeted me yesterday is vanishing in a late winter's mist. Early in the afternoon, I arrive at the train station to find Rosanne and John and Danny waiting near their track, weighted down with two guitars, numerous bags of luggage, and a blue satchel—Danny's—that I will soon learn is loaded with cash from the Albisgüetli show. Last night's bassist and drummer have jetted back to America, leaving Rosanne and John to their acoustic leg in Munich and Cologne. For those of you keeping score at home, John will split off to return to Jake and New York after Cologne.

The train to Munich boards, so I follow the trio to its first-class compartment before I break away to find a seat in second class. Danny offers to trade tickets with me should I want to interview Rosanne en route to Germany. They anticipate a pleasant Sunday ride through the Alps.

The train glides from Zurich's main station while I settle into my seat with a newspaper. The sun finally disappears behind a blanket of gray. Gathering power for its ascent into the mountains, the train passes dull industrial areas that contrast with the twinkly Zurich that enchanted me last night from my Albisgüetli perch. In time, snow appears on the embankment and in the fields and hills beyond. On both sides of the train, unusual tracts of brown huts come into view. They are *Schreber garten*, community vegetable gardens dotted with well-kept sheds that appear more like small homes with their pretty window curtains, swept walkways, and small chimneys puffing smoke.

Soon majestic peaks emerge from the mist, framing a succession of scrubbed towns and more of the curious gardens. I put down my newspaper, pick up my briefcase, and negotiate six or seven cars on my way to first class. When I arrive, John is stretched out on a bench while opposite him Rosanne dozes and Danny pages through a guidebook to Germany. In a few minutes, a conductor with a stern face tries to send me back to my place among the proletariat, but the trio in unison comes to my defense. The woman flashes a withering glare at me and slides the glass door closed.

Rosanne sits with her back to the forward direction of the train and scans the passing scenery, pointing out particularly impressive mountains and sprawling lakes. Our stop for passengers in Rorschach invites wisecracks about paint splattered on the station walls and whether the lake in the distance appears to John to be a lake or not. John pulls out his phone to shoot video to send back home, and Rosanne passes around photos from her appearance in Zurich years earlier. Soon she returns to her survey of the outside, occasionally slipping on her glasses to check if there's been word from Carrie, Jake, or his nanny.

We need no border agents out of some noir European film to tell us we're in Germany. The hard voice crackling over the intercom immediately makes us forget the mellower German spoken in Switzerland. "I can understand this German better," says Rosanne, referring to the sharper enunciation we hear. This blast of cold, hard German reminds me of the never-ending reels of Second World War documentaries I've watched since childhood. John looks down to his side and deadpans, "Imagine a Jew's perspective." I probably would have thought more about the mixed feelings of a Jew traveling in a nation whose leaders once tried to decimate his people, but the German on the speaker switches to English and ignites an unexpected commotion.

"To continue to Munich, you must board the train on the opposite track," the voice orders. Outside, conductors bark commands while passengers swarm across the platform like scared ducks. Evidently, the other train is primed to depart. We exchange confused looks and immediately begin pulling down cases from the rack above. How we avoid smacking them on each other's heads, I don't know, but like John, Paul, George, and Ringo in one of their 1960s comedies, we careen out of the car and onto the platform. I dash along the side of the train to fetch my bags, hoping that I won't be separated from the subject of this book.

As it happens, I pluck my bags and coats from second class in time to help the others with their luggage. I pause for a moment, though, before I do. Shouldn't I merely *observe* while Rosanne and company lug their stuff onto the new train? But there's no time for a crisis of ethics. So, like those slippery wild animal documentarians who stage bloody fights in the bush for the benefit of their films, I influence events, grabbing the bags and pulling them onto the crowded train.

All of a sudden, we are in that noir European film. The conductor who had glared at me earlier appears in the door and announces, "Ulm," which sounds to us like the French "un." The door rattles shut. There is no first class, only one seat for Rosanne in steerage. And for John, Danny, and me, places among suitcases stacked halfway to the ceiling. Danny glances at me. "Did she say, 'Un'?" he asks.

"Sounds like it," I respond.

"I assume she means get off in 'Un' and transfer to Munich," he says hopefully.

"Sounds like it."

We see no stop for "Un" on the map posted to the wall, but of greater concern is the movement of the train in the opposite direction of the one we just left. Resignation sets in. Rosanne, John, and Danny have just lost their idyllic train ride across the Alps, and I my momentary spot in first class. John takes a seat on his suitcase, and Danny leans against the stair railing that leads down to the car where Rosanne has found a seat. The men look like two army privates who just lost their weekend pass. Rosanne is wedged among three strangers. Still regaining her strength in the wake of brain surgery, the mad scramble has drained her. She naps and gazes out the window and naps again, occasionally checking her phone.

We learn that a transfer in "Ulm" will take us to Munich and that the opposite direction has somehow become the correct direction. We will change direction at least two more times in the course of the journey to Ulm, the birthplace of Albert Einstein. In Ulm, first-class space awaits, only this time they will have to share with one other person, a balding man in a burgundy sweater who will peck at his laptop throughout the journey.

The train has just pulled away from Ulm when chat turns to *The List*. Both John and Danny worry that Rosanne can't or won't articulate why she wants to do the album. Back on the first train, John was playing cuts for the album to everybody's liking, but every album needs a story, so he and Danny double-team her to find out how she will tender hers.

The man behind the laptop peeks up from his work. He seems to recognize Rosanne, but his eyes return to the blue screen.

Everyone agrees that it doesn't matter whether the sheet of paper turns up or not, that the spirit of the list is governing the project, and that's heavy enough. John asserts that it's got to be about Rosanne's heritage: the records she heard her father play in the living room when she lay in her bedroom at his Hendersonville house, or the songs she watched him deliver onstage when she toured with him in the 1970s. Rosanne considers John while the wheels rumble over the tracks. She seems somewhat uneasy with the notion that her father didn't merely hand her the list, but that—as John suggests—he poured the music over her. Anointed her? It may be too much to accept.

I keep waiting for the man with the laptop to join the discussion, to argue against a song chosen for the album or to defend Rosanne from the double team. Instead, he merely looks up quizzically from time to time and then looks down again.

Paying little attention to the man in the burgundy sweater, Rosanne cites the essay she wrote for Annie Leibovitz's book, which, she says to John and Danny, essentially explains her thoughts on heritage. "The roots of my longing and passion go deep, into my early childhood, I suppose," she had written, "when the imprint of my father on my little-girl's brain contained the shape of his guitar, the keening of his voice, the beat of his melodies, and his back, turned away from me and toward the spotlight. There is something about that image that speaks of love, and the unknowable, and endless travel, and the manifest soul. There is nothing in music that moves me more than this. . . . My own body is shaped nearly like a Martin D-28, my voice links to the deepest recesses of my heart, by way of a touch of his DNA and my own rocky experience, and I am part of a tradition, which is the last stop before timelessness."

Had she recited this missive as we journey in the train, I suspect the discussion would be over.

Three dates await Rosanne in Germany. She's never toured here before now, although in October 2008 she appeared at the "Century of Song" festival in Essen with Joe Henry and Billy Bragg. Rosanne found a free-flowing exchange of musical ideas that inspired her to return, but she also embraces the notion that Germany completes a circle more than thirty years in the making. In 1978 Rosanne recorded her first album in Munich, for Ariola, an imprint affiliated with the Bertlesmann media empire. The release marked her solo debut in the music industry, a moment in her career ironically spattered with regret.

Before we left for the European tour, she told me in her New York home that the circle began in London in 1976. Her father was traveling around America as one of the nation's major bicentennial symbols, and she was living in England, working for CBS, Columbia Records' parent company. London had been an escape from the doldrums of Nashville and the anguish of an unrequited love. "I had been in love with Randy Scruggs, and Randy Scruggs was going to get married," she recalled. "Randy and I had never had a relationship, but I had this dream of Randy. My heart was just broken. So *that* plus the idea of moving to London at the age of twenty [pointed the way]. So Dad was going along with it. 'Okay, this is great.' He helped me get a job at CBS on Trafalgar Square." She soon fell into the company of a few American ex-patriots, and she also ran with a pack of native wags who loved to play on her naïveté. The Britons she knew persuaded her to eat black pudding by telling her it was made of cherries and convinced her that the Queen of England's favorite dish was corgi.

Breaking from her British adventure, Rosanne flew to Nashville for a visit. Planning on a short stay, she was surprised to find her father demanding that she stay for good. "I said, 'What do you mean?' I had just turned twenty-one. He said, 'That's long enough, that's too far away, you have to come home now.' Then I argued a little bit. I said, 'I have to go back and pack my apartment.' [He said], 'No. Call someone to pack it up for you.' He was adamant. He would just not let me go back. So I didn't argue. I was twenty-one. I couldn't. But he was so authoritative about it, and he was never like that. Then he told me later that he was afraid that he'd never see me again, that I would move to Europe and I would never come back. So I did. I called my girlfriends. They packed up my apartment. I broke my lease. I moved back to Nashville. I enrolled at Vanderbilt. I was so depressed. I just hated my life, just hated it. It was not a good time to suddenly become meek and give in to my parents."

Surely the irony of an absentee father demanding that she stay close to his home was not lost on Rosanne, but she resented more than anything her status as the oldest person in the sophomore class at Vanderbilt. "Then," she continued, "I said, 'I can't do this. I can't live in Nashville, and I can't go to Vanderbilt.' So I moved to L.A., and I went to [the Lee Strasberg Theatre and Film Institute], which was great, but then I also realized deep in my heart that I was not cut out for acting. Although I loved method acting for the same reason I now love performance and singing—it's kind of the same thing to me—I realized I was not equipped to go on auditions, didn't have thick enough skin. So that was really troubling to me. . . . I was really weighing these things in my heart. 'Is this something I can make a life out of?'"

At the time, Rosanne had also added songwriting to her list of career possibilities. Obviously she knew Randy Scruggs and his writing credits, but she had also met his younger brother, Steve Scruggs, who had played with Randy in the Earl Scruggs Revue. "He was a very dear friend, and he would come by and we would write songs together and play songs to each other and try to be good songwriters." She had even made a few demo recordings of her songs.

More than a year after Rosanne had returned from London, a record promotion woman based in Germany, whom Rosanne knew through her father and through her internship in London, invited her to Munich for Christmas. Renata Damm opened her apartment in Munich to Rosanne and escorted the young woman through the city's social life. Still hungry for Europe, and now grappling with her feelings for a married man back in America named Rodney Crowell, Rosanne was happy to be in Renata's care. Mingling at an Ariola Records party, Renata—with Rosanne at her side—mentioned to an A&R executive that Rosanne wrote songs. The man asked for demos. "So I sent them, and they signed me," she recalled. "They wanted me to make a record, and I thought if I was going to make a record, doing it in Europe would be a really good way to begin. Get out of Dad's spotlight a little bit and experiment on my own. I was really shy, really painfully shy, and I thought if it didn't work out, then nobody would notice."

After the Christmas party, Rosanne returned to America and looked up the intriguing Crowell, whom she knew had played with and written for Emmylou Harris. "I liked what he had done on Emmy's records and always saw his name and thought I liked his songs. I don't even think I knew what a producer did so much. I kind of did, because I knew [Dad's producer] Bob Johnston, . . . but I thought, 'If he [writes songs] he can probably produce.' And so I called him, and I was so nervous. 'Do you think you could produce?' And he said, 'Well, I've never produced anything, but let's talk about it.' So he said he would do it. And we did part of it at House of Cash, and part of it at another studio. And it was really great. We worked together really well. I kind of fell in love with him. He was married. I kept it to myself. And then [Ariola] bought it. They liked the demo, but didn't want him to produce the whole record."

So Rosanne followed her demos back to Munich and moved in with Renata. "It was a few days before we were going to start, and I couldn't get out of bed," she recalled. "I just couldn't think. I was so depressed. Renata got worried and took me to this doctor and said, 'She can't get out of bed.' And the doctor talked to me a little

Rosanne in Renata Damm's apartment, 1978.

bit, and then he said, 'She's depressed.' And I didn't have enough self-awareness to know what was going on, but then I realized that I was about to make . . . I almost cry when I think about it . . . this big life-changing decision. If I made a record, that was it. I wasn't going back to acting school. I was going to be making records for my life, and I couldn't. It was so hard to take the first step."

At the mention of this turn in her life, Rosanne was not "almost" crying. She was in tears. She darted from her kitchen table to re-trieve a tissue from the counter and buried her eyes in it. "It didn't get to me until it was crunch time, until it was time to go to work," she continued. "Up until then, I was like, 'Oh, I'm an international film star or whatever. They're flying me to Europe.' It was fun. And then when it was time to do it, that's when it hit me. . . . This was an absolute fork. Whatever path I took, there was no turning back. This was it. I knew that. Isn't that funny? And I can't say I never regretted it.

"There were times I thought, 'This is too hard.' If I could go back, maybe I wouldn't have done it."

I was intrigued. "You never wanted to be famous?" I asked.

"No, that was the worst thing that could happen to me. . . ."

" . . . because you knew the price of fame."

"Yes. Your marriage broke up. You did drugs. You stayed away from home all the time. Your mother went insane. And not only that, my mother had so much anxiety about me becoming a musician, and she didn't withhold it."

This was news to me. But it made perfect sense. With her father's example flush in her face, why wouldn't she second-guess her choice, regret it even?

"I wanted to write songs for people," she said, still brushing aside tears. "When I first started writing songs, I would always look at who the songwriters were when I was living in Nashville in my late teens. The singer just seemed to me a vehicle for whoever the songwriter was. Like a great Harlan Howard song, that was who I respected. Not the guy who was singing it. And also, there was no spotlight to it. It just seemed perfect for me. And there's prestige among people you want to have prestige with: other songwriters.

"So being faced with this other option in Germany [was daunting]. I knew what I was doing when I made the demos, but I was still playing 'make the demos.' But then when I was actually faced with going into the studio to make the record, then it was terrifying. But I liked Europe. Part of what made me go ahead and take the step was I had already lived in London for six months at that point. I'd been in Munich a lot. And I liked being in Europe. I would have moved to Europe. And I thought, 'If I'm going to do this, it will be perfect. I'll just stay here.'"

As it happened, she stayed in Munich only long enough to make the record. "After about three days [in bed], I went into the studio, and it ended up being a painful experience. They assigned a German producer to me. Bernie Vonficht was his name, and it was the height of Donna Summer. Donna Summer had just made ["I Feel Love"] in Munich, and so this was a big, big deal to the German record industry, and a lot of German artists were trying to do American-sounding disco records. That's where Bernie's experience was, and so I went into the studio, and I would sing in a folk kind of accent. And he kept trying to correct my pronunciation, and I finally said to him, 'But I'm American. I know how to say these words.' So we just kept butting heads and butting heads, and then he wanted me to do this song. I had a sense of what I wanted to do—I mean, not as clear as I got later on, but I had an idea of what was me and what was good and what I really wanted to sing, and I did have some integrity. Even at the age of twenty-one, twenty-two, I had a sense of musical integrity.

"So he brings this song into the studio that he wants me to record. He said, 'This is going to be a huge hit.' Well, I absolutely hated the song, hated it. I said, 'I can't do that.' We had this enormous argument about it. I'm a kid. And he said, 'But this is a huge hit.' I said, 'But I don't care. . . .' So he stormed out of the studio. He was very, very angry, and he told me what time to show up the next day, and when I showed up, he had told the musicians to show up three hours before me, and he had recorded a track for that song. And he said, 'Now you will sing on the track.' And I said, 'No, I'm not doing it.' And he got furious with me. And he said, 'I'll put my own voice on this track because this is going to be a big hit.' I said, 'You go ahead and do that.' Well, he did. And it became a huge hit. And when I went back to promote the record, he was there at his own fan table with his big hit record and buttons with his picture on it. It was so funny. And he said, 'I told you it would be a hit.'"

Unlike Vonficht's record, Rosanne's self-titled debut flared up briefly. Hampered by her uncertain vocals and the shrinking taste for country-folk music in Germany, the record soon dissolved into

Rosanne with Bernie Vonficht in Munich, 2009

obscurity. Today collectors don't just walk into used-record shops and find the album. It's a certified rarity.

If Germany failed to develop a taste for Rosanne, the sentiment was reciprocated. "I built up a lot of time in Munich," she told me. "I was going back and forth from L.A. to Munich all the time. Eleven-hour flight. I had it down pat. But the idea of living there permanently? Munich seemed a little too hard for me to do because of the language thing, although I was getting better. I could order a taxi and a meal in German. But also then I started to feel the pull of Rodney. He started writing me when I was there. He wrote me a lot of letters when I was in Munich. So that was very attractive to me. I think if it hadn't been for Rodney, I would have stayed in Munich much longer. At one point then, I flew back. The record was done. I flew to L.A. The day I got in I saw Rodney, and that was it. I stayed with him from then on. By this time he was split up with his wife."

Because the album sank quietly into the subterranean, Rosanne never got the call to tour Germany. Even in the verdant 1980s she stayed away, having little taste for touring anywhere. But in these new days of March 2009 she tempts the past.

After our discombobulating train journey to Munich, she checks into the St. George's Hotel and quickly dresses to meet Renata Damm, whom she has invited for dinner at the hotel, which, though only a block from the gritty central train station, is one of the finest in the city. Dressed in a leg-hugging skirt, Rosanne invites a trip down memory lane with Renata, who appears to be in her seventies. They laugh about sparring with Bernie Vonficht, riding bikes through Munich's bustling streets, and Rosanne's fling with an Israeli singer while Renata was traveling elsewhere in Germany.

There is substantial talk about Tina Turner's concert last night, which Renata, still flush with music industry friends, attended. With every adjective that Renata spins recounting a spectacular scene change or costume change, Rosanne grows quieter. After a brief but unavoidable consideration of Tina's legs, which elicits nods from John and Danny, Rosanne finally interjects. "I just couldn't do it," she exclaims. "Work like that at the age of seventy." It's a confession that surprises no one. She half-seriously pouts that Tina has probably sucked all of the concert dollars out of Munich.

As it happens, Tina has left plenty for Rosanne. A half-hour before showtime the Muffathalle, tonight's venue, is filling quickly.

Situated in a dell along the Isar River, whose alpine waters rush to the Danube, the Muffathalle neighbors the famed Deutschesmuseum and the Kulturzentrum am Gasteig, two of Munich's cultural

A poster for the show hanging outside the Muffathalle.

landmarks. So for tonight, Rosanne dwells in a hub of German intellectual activity.

No cowboy hats bob up and down among the crowd, but I do
spy a stray beret and more than a few leather jackets. Lit by scarlet
lights that cascade down the black walls, the men and women of
Munich file through industrial-sized stage door entrances in hushed
tones. A few carry old Rosanne Cash albums that they hope she
will sign, while others carefully hold glasses of beer and wine as they
shimmy between rows searching for their seats.

The crowd is subdued in German fashion, so it must be a quartet
of British expatriates who, behind me, rise above the din. Four

women who left their husbands at home for the evening have an animated discussion about their day's work at the European Patent Office. I assume they represent a legion of female fans that Rosanne amassed in the 1980s. They are about her age. But I'm wrong. They know country music—two of them have trekked to Nashville on holidays—but none of them, I will learn in the bar later, own a Rosanne Cash disc or can name one of her hits. They tell me in no uncertain terms that the aura of Johnny Cash has drawn them to the Muffathalle.

If Rosanne were with me when I learn the women's motivations, she might nod with resignation. "I always get that percentage that comes to try to see my dad. I go, 'He's not here.' . . . [They try] to look through me to see him or are so obsessed with him that they will do anything to get even a little bit close. Sometimes I think those people are figures of my subconscious, just come to torment me. And sometimes they are just sweet. They just really loved my dad."

The expatriates of course have never seen Rosanne perform, and, I gather, neither have most of the other visitors. It will be a first encounter all around.

She walks on the stage and straight into the opening bars of "Runaway Train," her number-one hit from 1988. With its haunting

The British expatriates (l to r), Marian MacFarland, Jane Diel, Maria Home-wood, Marion Pugh.

images of dark curves and lanterns swaying, it brings Mississippi darkness to the Munich night and promises that tonight will at least be somewhat retrospective, a nod to the city that gave birth to her recording life, no matter how mixed her feelings are regarding that chapter of her story.

The Germans watch Rosanne's and John's every move as if they were tightrope walkers. Utterly respectful and engaged, they save their applause until the last tone fades from John's guitar, so different than the Zurich experience.

And when Rosanne speaks, the crowd warms up to her even more. She reveals that this is the first performance ever in Munich and recounts the story of her first recording. They understand her English much better than the Swiss did, and they show it by smiling in satisfaction over Munich's seminal role in her career. By way of an introduction to 2006's "Radio Operator," which refers to her parents' love affair, she explains that her father was stationed in the air force at nearby Landsberg in the early 1950s. She chokes up as she tells the story, and the fans love her for it, and love that she knows Landsberg.

Early in the evening an eerie ball of manufactured smoke wanders around the stage, proving to be the only contrived element of the show. Finally, somebody just switches it off, leaving Rosanne and John alone onstage to motor through a liberal helping of selections from 2003's *Rules of Travel* and 2006's *Black Cadillac*, a smattering of old hits like "Blue Moon with Heartache" and "Seven Year Ache," and one or two Johnny Cash hits. A voice calls out for "I Still Miss Someone," Johnny's 1958 recording. It momentarily stuns and then irritates Rosanne, but at least the request is for one of her father's that she actually performs, not, say, "Flushed from the Bathroom of Your Heart" or "A Boy Named Sue." She complies, and as she sings the yearning lyric a soft purple spotlight falls on an empty space next to her, a reminder of the one whom we all miss.

Rosanne answers her final encore with a withering cover of Bobbie Gentry's "Ode to Billie Joe," which stretches out every thread in the lurid story. To me, there's no mistaking each stitch in the narrative as Rosanne delivers it, but later one of the British women asks, "Was it the *bay-bee* that she threw off the bridge?"

The houselights rise, and Rosanne returns to her dressing room. Soon, she emerges to meet autograph seekers who have gathered at the foot of the stage. But as she signs her name for the first time, she sees Renata slicing through the throng, leading Bernie Vonficht. There is nothing to do but embrace him.

"That was great," she'll say later. "I mean, I had always had kind of this little chip about him because we didn't end in a good way. We ended in a battle over that song that he eventually did himself. So, to see him, it was just like getting a thorn removed from your leg or something. It was great. He was so sweet. He was in tears. You could tell he'd lived those thirty-one years [since our recording]

Signing autographs after the Muffathalle performance.

in his own body too, you see that and you have to respect it. He was just so kind. It was a washing away of anything negative that had been left over."

After Rosanne, John, and Danny have left, I sit in the bar that adjoins the Muffathalle with the British women, and we analyze Barack Obama, compare health care systems, and attempt to make sense of the Willie Nelson phenomenon. Finally I ask what they thought of the show, and it is raven-haired Marion, the daughter of Irish immigrants, who leads the commentary. She was riveted by "Ode to Billie Joe" and relished "I Still Miss Someone," but she appreciates more than anything witnessing Rosanne's return to a place of origin, and she senses that the singer has touched new ground. "I felt like I was part of something special tonight," says Marion.

CHAPTER 10

Take These Chains

Munich to Cologne is a long ride. They fly. I take the train, a 350-mile ride. When I arrive, I am feverish and cramped with aches and pains. In front of the train station, the massive Cologne Cathedral looms over the plaza, but I am too sick to walk inside and take in this necessary religious landmark. Hotel bed and pain relief are on my mind.

Rosanne plays tonight at Kulturkirche, a place tucked away in a residential sector north of the city center, where neighbors have been known to call the police when the music cranks. It could be loud music, though, that cures me. I imagine Rosanne and John's playing flowing through me, causing my heart to race, uncorking my adrenaline, and expelling my illness. As corny as it sounds, I imagine needing the music.

As it turns out, all I need is the pain reliever and a bowl of thick vegetable soup from a Turkish carryout near my hotel.

I make it in time to Kulturkirche, which, surprisingly, is actually a church. I assume that it has been decommissioned and is used strictly for cultural events, and the groups of patrons walking to their pews carrying beers and doughy pretzels seem to confirm as much. But as I gaze up into the neo-Gothic apse, I spot two Bible verses painted on the wall, a hint that perhaps I am wrong. I will learn later that Kulturkirche is Kulturkirche only when artists like Rosanne visit. The rest of the time it is Lutherkirche, a favorite place of worship for many residents of Cologne.

Tonight Rosanne again sparks the fire with "Runaway Train," whose mystery only deepens in the dim church, its every verse formulated with the potency of an entire Jimmie Rodgers song. *We're lighting the fuses and counting to three / And what are the choices for those who remain / The sign of the cross on a runaway train.* She beautifully acts the song, extending her arms toward the audience as if to embrace the lyrics in a lover's dance, raising her face to the sky to sing for the ancient ghosts that haunt her "Runaway Train." Rosanne's passion charges her vocals and dictates every expression and body movement. It is its own performance.

The third performance is John's. His abilities cannot be overstated. He draws from his acoustic guitar the depth and dynamism of three instruments. First in Munich and now tonight in Cologne, one cannot say that the show is lesser in the absence of a full band. John *is* a full band, accented by Rosanne's occasional rhythm guitar. He supplies snappy riffs, chunky chords, tender melodies, and pensive bridges. In his hands, the guitar goes electric, thumps like a bass, and bleats like a pedal steel. When the duo tumbles into 1987's "Tennessee Flat Top Box," whose trademark is its delicious and intricate guitar runs, John brings to mind country guitar legend Grady Martin, if not Rosanne's old-time crush Randy Scruggs, who actually performed it on her record. John is probably technically superior to both of them.

A lot rests on John's shoulders. He beefs up the musical presentation so fans don't feel cheated at shelling out thirty euros for the show and gives Rosanne the space to bring her songwriting to the fore. I worry that Rosanne will stagger without him in Berlin. He is to fly home tomorrow to be with Jake.

Tonight, they shine together.

Kulturkirche.

But curiously, there's just enough rebelliousness in both of them
to find ways to repel their audience. Although they don't patently
snub their fans in the fashion of, say, Jerry Lee Lewis or Amy Wine-
house, they give them reason to scratch their heads. It uncoiled into
view in Munich, and it does again tonight in Cologne. Feeling the
magnanimity that grows from an appreciative crowd, Rosanne offers
to take requests, but she freezes over when the suggestions displease
her. In Cologne a woman hollers for "I Walk the Line," to which
Rosanne responds with a curt "no." When somebody suggests "I Still
Miss Someone," she happily accepts. Of course, she regularly performs
"I Still Miss Someone," but how is the poor Walk-the-Line frau in
the front row who requested "I Walk the Line"—who is probably
feeling rejected and embarrassed—supposed to know that Rosanne

finds it too clichéd a choice and probably believes it to be an inferior example of song craft next to "I Still Miss Someone"?

"That's such a tricky area," Rosanne tells me after the show. "There are some songs of my dad's that I can embody authentically: 'I Still Miss Someone,' 'Tennessee Flat Top Box'—clearly, I had a number-one record on it—'Big River.' There's some I couldn't touch with a ten-foot pole, that just would be wrong. So, those people that ask for those, I think they sometimes do it to be provocative. Sometimes they'll say 'I Walk the Line' just to be provocative and kind of tweak me a little, knowing that I'm not going to do it."

In Munich, when Rosanne invited requests, a fan cried for her 1981 number-one hit "My Baby Thinks He's a Train," but she rejected that too, like a center in basketball slapping down a shot. The song would appear to stray from her oeuvre these days, but Rosanne has not exactly been keeping Germany apprised of her oeuvre these past thirty years. It's as if she expected the fan to know that "My Baby Thinks He's a Train" is too Nashville or ties her to an image that she'd rather not project in 2009. And she appeared unfazed that her terse reply might have offended him.

John whispered to the Munich audience that he would like Rosanne to sing "My Baby Thinks He's a Train," but in Cologne he joins Rosanne in this paradoxical beating back of solicited requests. Not surprisingly, somebody in the congregation suggests 1993's "The Wheel," a Rosanne composition that critic Alanna Nash once said "showed a new maturity and diversity of songwriting." Rosanne seems intrigued and willing, but John scotches it, claiming that he can't play it to his satisfaction, although he probably could play a passable accompaniment in his sleep.

John also has an early flight in the morning, and he obviously needs the show to end. I say "obviously" because he is unabashedly communicating his need in front of the Kulturkirche crowd. And—

despite my observations about the requests—the crowd is unabashedly communicating its need to hold on to Rosanne. Her final three songs in the regular set mesmerize the audience: a rocking "Sea of Heartbreak" from *The List*, the exhilarating "Seven Year Ache," and *Black Cadillac*'s "Dreams Are Not My Home."

John and Rosanne both see an encore coming, so they hurry away and then hurry back with what could be a plan to calm the mass so it will release them to the night. When they return, they slip into the scintillating "Ode to Billie Joe," which only ignites the crowd. The song dies out in a wild gale of applause, and John turns and makes for the wings while Rosanne drinks in the appreciation. But she summons him back to his perch, and when he turns, there is a grimace on his face. He plods back and dutifully launches into the elegant "God Is in the Roses." His impatience with the delay is palpable, and whether the crowd is reading it or not and allowing it to color how they feel about Rosanne, I don't know. I do know John projects pure disgust when Rosanne asks her man to stay for one more. She sheepishly turns to the crowd and explains John's travel plans. And then she wistfully, willingly unfurls "500 Miles," welling up when she sings, *Teardrops fell on Mama's note / When I read the things she wrote.*

In the Kulturkirche vestibule there is no sign of the contempt that Rosanne showed for the errant requests, and John is packing up guitars and grabbing a quick bite to eat in the church library, which tonight is a makeshift dressing room. She greets the fans who want her to sign their photos, albums, and books. It's an obligatory task, reminiscent of the country music circuit, where fans expect all but the most popular George Strait–type artists to appear after the show and greet them. I suppose also it's a form of surrender: these German venues are porous, allowing no hiding place from those who really want to meet her. So she and Danny might as well manage it as best they can. They have grown leery of many of the fans, the ones who step forward with a stack of photographs that inevitably show up on auction websites within days and those who produce Johnny Cash memorabilia for her signature. I flinch when I see a woman nosing into the crowd wielding a paperback copy of her father's second autobiography. In Munich a small group of opportunists who hadn't seen the show charged in to the Muffathalle with their collectors' items just as Rosanne emerged to sign autographs and greet Bernie Vonficht.

Rosanne's German fans are mostly subdued, but a few glazed stares and painted-on smiles may be windows to their tendencies or, in a kinder light, just expressions of intense fascination with the core of American music that Rosanne represents, what jazzman and Chicago hipster Mezz Mezzrow called the European search for the "way straight back to the good and solid source." One man hustles behind Rosanne as she leaves the vestibule and walks through the dark courtyard to the church library. He wants her to bring a photo inside for John's signature. So the photo is carried inside and placed in front of John. He scrawls his name along the border and underneath in big black letters writes, "DO NOT SELL ON E-BAY."

In the morning, after John has departed for New York, Rosanne and Danny pile into a car that will take them to Essen, an industrial city north of Cologne that is the birthplace of Nazi munitions maker Alfried Krupp and former West German president Gustav Heinemann. She plans to visit a naturopathic doctor who has helped her in her recovery from brain surgery. While we drive, I am anxious to engage her reflections on the tour thus far, but for some reason on this late winter morning her 1990 album *Interiors* simmers below the surface. The album is a crucial part of her legacy, the moment when she abandoned once and for all the Nashville machine

Rosanne and Danny in Essen.

and pursued her own course. If *The List* is an acknowledgment of her past, *Interiors* was a decided departure from it.

To Rosanne, the album embodies a roiling mix of experiences: rebirth, separation, transition, betrayal, confusion, regret. So it's no wonder that the mere mention of the album incites deep discussion. It crops up this morning as we discuss the audience requests. She mentions that wherever she goes she meets specific groups of people who are intensely loyal to it. "I don't mean to stereotype, but a lot of them are gay men who really like *Interiors*. It is interesting—that particular record draws its own crowd."

Memories of making the album, selling the album to Columbia, and touring on the album come alive and ignite a passionate conversation that draws in Danny and would have drawn in the German driver too had the journey lasted longer than it did.

"I had just had four number-one records with *King's Record Shop* [in 1987 and 1988]," she remembers. "I had built collateral in the industry to do something that I wanted to do, to do an artistic project. And I did it. And [the label] shook hands and showed me the door. Like when Springsteen turned in *Nebraska*, they didn't say, 'Oh, sorry, we can't play you anymore.'"

To clarify, Columbia's Nashville office waved good-bye to Rosanne, not the label itself. She still had her Columbia contract, but her marketing and A&R support moved to New York.

"It was like I was walking into this corner," she continues. "And then there was no way out. The country music industry is not built to allow artistic experimentation. It is built to repeat what was successful. And I didn't want to do that. I felt like a fraud. . . . I wrote two songs on *King's Record Shop*. I don't want to be doing this. So I follow what I want to do. I think in another part of the industry I would have been allowed, and it would have been given space and credit and validity. And it wasn't there. And so clearly that's not the branch of the industry I belong in, right? If I want to be an artist who experiments and really stretches, then that's not where I should be. It's like if you want to really see a lot of culture, you shouldn't live in Ames, Iowa."

Whether Rosanne knows it or not, she is channeling the legendary bandleader Artie Shaw. Frustrated with the industry's demand that he play "Begin the Beguine" every night, he lay down his clarinet in the 1950s and rarely if ever picked it up again before his death in 2004. He complained, "I got to a place where they said, 'Stop, don't grow any more.' That's like telling a pregnant woman, 'Stop, don't get more pregnant.'" Rosanne's thoughts may have been running along such lines when she began contemplating her retreat from Nashville.

"It was painful," she exclaims. "It was like a divorce. I remember three months into the release of the record, I was sitting on a plane, and I felt devastated. I saw that they weren't doing anything for this record that I had poured everything into. I was just sitting there by myself thinking, 'What am I going to do? How do I take my life back?' And so I just got this overwhelming feeling that I had to ask them to transfer me, and I knew I was sacrificing *Interiors*. It was too late. It was three and a half, four months [after the release]. So I went back, and I talked to [manager] Will Botwin, and I talked to Rodney, I talked to some people I trust. I talked to my dad. He said, 'Go for it. You don't need to be here.' He said, 'You need to be in New York.' They all said that. So I went into that meeting by myself at Sony with all the top guys in Nashville, and it was over in twenty minutes. I swear to God, they shook my hand and said, 'We'll miss you.' That was it."

I ask her if she really wanted them to say, "Stay, Rosanne. We'll work it out."

"Thinking about it now, how I felt, I was dizzy. I think I held the door when I walked out. I was dizzy, it was shocking. I went, 'Now what am I going to do?' So they transfer me to New York. I go meet with Donny Ienner. He's nice, he wants me, but by this time they can't market *Interiors*, it's over. It was nice it got nominated for a Grammy, because there was really nothing behind it."

But the years have been kind to *Interiors*, I observe as the car speeds along the German highway. It's one of only three Rosanne Cash albums that Sony has remastered and rereleased, ironically.

"David Byrne told me that he knew my work before," she replies, "but that *Interiors* introduced me to a lot of people that didn't know me from before, and it legitimized me in a way for them.

"I'm philosophical about these things," she continues. "I think that they happen, that you set it up, some unconscious part of yourself sets it up and things move in a way. Not that everything that happens is supposed to happen. But I think it was the right thing. But like I said, there was a lot of bad blood. Nobody was in that

Still in Essen.

meeting with me, and I knew that they didn't want that record. So it became my fault. I left them. It was childish. It happened to co-incide with me and Rodney breaking up, so that really shattered people's little ideal. You know, we were a golden couple. It was on the front page of [every newspaper] arts section when we split.

"I remember Robert Christgau wrote a review saying it was a divorce record, and my jaw hit my chest, and I got scared, like he knew something that I didn't know. And he did. I mean, I didn't know I was going to get divorced when I made that record."

So she knew something that she didn't know?

"Exactly. But I had a little running patter in that tour. I did a pretty, for me, serious tour after *Interiors*, and it was with a trio. And I had this little running joke: that my parents heard *Interiors*, and my dad was like, 'That was a great record.' And my mom was like, 'What's wrong?' She chuckles. 'Are you okay?'"

I ask Rosanne if the label had given her any sign during production that she was veering away from their expectations.

"I didn't communicate with them that much. They didn't hear a lot when I was making it. I went in. It was very insular. I did a lot of preproduction with [guitarist] Steuart Smith. Steuart and [engineer] Roger Nichols were my two guys, and I just had these ideas about sonics. I recorded it on a twenty-four-track Trident board. I recorded it analog. So I conveyed to Roger in sonic terms . . . what I wanted it to sound like. I talked to Steuart about arrangements, about how stripped down I wanted it to be, that I didn't want a full drum kit on anything. When we finally got in the studio, Steuart and [bass player] Michael Rhodes said, 'Come on, can't we put a full drum kit on "All Come True?," which didn't even make the final record actually. . . . So I hung this sign above the studio door that says, 'Abandon thought all ye who enter here.' It was very insulated. It was just these guys and me. I had baby Carrie, and I took her to the studio a lot. The label didn't hear much until I was done. And then I called them in, I can't remember who the A&R guy was, and we played them a few tracks, and I remember playing 'What We Really Want' to him, and at the end of it he said, 'We can't do anything with that.' He literally said that. 'We can't do anything with that.'

"I wasn't defeated, but I was shaken. I thought, 'Well, he's wrong.' And he was right. But who knows why. It was a fait accompli at that point."

From the front seat, Danny interjects, "It's such a difficult, strained relationship when it comes to the art of music and the commercial marketing of that art. I'm not defending the industry. It's just so complicated because it's not a natural relationship."

"It isn't a natural relationship, you are right," she replies. "And I do have sympathy for their side of it. From their side, I had just had four number-one records, right? I was starting to build an empire for them, and then I deliver them something that is the antithesis of what they want. So I get it."

Says Danny, "Everyone just repeats the successes until something breaks the mold, but it's not a decision that breaks the mold. It's usually a radical rising of something that creates a new popularity."

I add that the artist who continues to follow the formula finds that the formula peters out.

"That's right," agrees Rosanne.

And then Danny jumps back in. "Then they have to make a drastic unnatural move . . . "

" . . . or," interrupts Rosanne, "you make parodies of yourself for the rest of your life. Even [when I did] *King's Record Shop*—and I was still a young woman—I could see the future. I could see myself falling into this thing of having to do parodies of myself at the age of sixty."

Suddenly Rosanne jumps the track. She recognizes a bridge from her last visit in the fall and sees another link to her past. "You know, it's funny, if I hadn't done 'Century of Song,' we wouldn't be here right now. It just sparked something. It also sparked an idea about coming back to Germany, about being here thirty-plus years later and fulfilling that promise to myself."

Rosanne gazes at the farmland, which is just beginning to blush with green. The car turns off the autobahn and drops down into the valley that leads to Essen.

CHAPTER 11

Girl in the
North Country

When Rosanne tells me that she and John are working up a cover of "Girl from the North Country," which Bob Dylan recorded with her father in 1969, I have no idea that she and Dylan had brushed up against each other in the past. I guess I shouldn't be surprised: both she and John know Larry Campbell, who worked with Dylan early in this decade, and they rent an apartment to G. E. Smith, another alumnus of Dylan's band. In an alcove off Rosanne's living room, a telling series of photographs taken in the 1960s portray Johnny Cash towering over Dylan in conversation, much like that iconic picture of Lyndon B. Johnson leaning into Abe Fortas the day after he nominated the reluctant Fortas to the Supreme Court in 1965. The picture makes clear that only Cash could impress Bob Dylan.

But Rosanne's iteration of the Cash DNA once had a far more heart-racing effect on the folk troubadour. You might remember the Bob Dylan tribute concert at Madison Square Garden in 1993—dubbed "Bobfest" by Neil Young—for Sinéad O'Connor's face-off with segments of the audience who were offended that she'd recently ripped a photo of Pope John Paul II in two during a *Saturday*

Night Live appearance, but Rosanne remembers the show for entirely different reasons.

"There were not that many dressing rooms," she recalls. "I think there were eight women or six women in one dressing room; it was me and Sophie B. Hawkins and Sinéad O'Connor, Sheryl Crow. Sheryl Crow hadn't even started her own career yet; she was singing backup for Sinéad. And so she was in the dressing room too, and Shawn Colvin and Mary Chapin Carpenter. I think my dad and June had their own dressing room down the hall. . . . And George Harrison was there. It was a huge deal to everybody that George was there. John and I were not married yet, but John was there with me and at rehearsal. You know, I had done [a] Cinemax special with Carl Perkins and George [in 1985]. So that had been a few years before that. So at rehearsal, George was walking to the stage, and he saw me, and he said, 'Hi, Rosanne,' and I think that's why John married me . . . because George Harrison said hi to me! So funny.

"Anyway, so it's not long before the show, and some man comes to the dressing room and says, 'Bob wants to see you.' Well, at first I thought he said, 'John wants to see you.' So I didn't realize where I was going. I was already dressed, ready to go on. So he takes me to Bob's dressing room, and Bob was talking to someone and signing papers or something, so I stood and waited, and I thought, 'Oh, he didn't like something at rehearsal.' I even thought, 'He's going to kick me off the show because he didn't like how it sounded.' I was so nervous, and so he asked this person to leave, so we were alone in the room, and he says, 'You look very lovely.' And I still didn't get it. I was, 'Thank you.' And I'm waiting for him to say, 'But this song sucks. You're out!' And so that was kind of it. We talked for a few minutes. I said, 'Are you nervous?' He said, 'I wish I was nervous.' And then that was it, and I was so confused, and he didn't say I was kicked off, he didn't say anything about the song, so I walk out, walking down the hall, and I stop and I realize that he was flirting. So instead of going back to my dressing room, I went to my dad's dressing room. I said, 'Dad, I think Bob likes me.' And my dad said, 'Oh, I *know* he does.' . . . There was a little bit of alarm in his voice when he said, 'Oh, I *know* he does.' That was funny. It was a high-octane night. There was a lot of feelings floating around."

When Rosanne arrives in Berlin with nobody but Danny Kahn, a half-moon looks down on the city. The sprawling Tiergarten, which dominates the city center, is like a desert this Wednesday evening. A few cars fly down the broad 17 Juni strasse—named to commemorate the 1953 East Berlin uprising—but most of the businesspeople and tourists have long since returned to their homes and hotels for the evening.

Rosanne's show is scheduled for tomorrow at yet another still-functioning church, the Passionskirche, in what used to be East Berlin. It's uncertain just how Rosanne will adapt her show in John's absence, but she doesn't seem awfully worried about it, even though she has rarely played alone. In fact, when I ask, she can remember only two or three times when she's taken the stage without accompaniment. "I played Harvard Square [near Boston] last by myself, promoting a record. Actually, John was supposed to go with me, and he couldn't at the last minute, so I did that by myself. That was fine. I played." She chuckles at the memory. "When *The Wheel* came out, I played at a basement day care center in Brooklyn by myself, a couple hundred people or something. That was fun. But like I said, it's been a long time since I've done a whole show by myself.

"I can do it," she insists. "It makes me a little nervous, and I haven't done it in a really long time. And it's a whole different thing, clearly, because John adds so much. . . . For me to do it alone, it's

Signing autographs in Berlin.

just doing the songs. So that has to be enough. I have to make that enough.

"There are some [songs] I literally can't do. Like, I can't do 'Tennessee Flat Top Box.' I can't do 'Runaway Train' because of the way it's been reinvented; I don't know how to play it. I can do 'God Is in the Roses,' but just a simple folk song version of it. 'Seven Year Ache,' I can't do the lick, but I can certainly play it; it will take people longer to recognize the song if they would have known it."

In Cologne, John told me that Rosanne was perfectly capable of carrying the show on her own, but I can't imagine that she will reach the same heights without him.

Danny may have had his doubts too, because back in New York he contacted a few Berlin guitar players capable of embellishing Rosanne's act. In yet another example of the influence of new technology, Danny had merely visited the guitarist's websites to glimpse video of their playing, and he, in turn, had sent them audio files of Rosanne's songs. In the end, he invited a young player named Andreas Binder to show up at Passionskirche in the afternoon before the show to see how he might mesh with the visiting songstress.

In the morning, Rosanne betrays no concern about whether Andreas will work out or not. After a spa treatment in her hotel, she sets out along the tony Fredreichstrasse and visits boutiques that seem more like art galleries than clothiers, lingering in them for a distracting period of time. And then she comes upon the old Checkpoint Charlie, where she examines posters telling the history of the old East-West crossroads and buys an army beret and pins bearing iconic symbols of the Soviet Union from a grizzled vendor to bring home to Jake.

I arrive in the afternoon at Passionskirche to find Rosanne signing autographs and posing for photographs on the steps of the old church. When she finishes, she hurries in, drapes her coat on a nearby chair, and greets Andreas, who could pass for a young Robert Gordon of 1970s rockabilly revival fame. Her signature probing grin is on high volume.

While Andreas tunes his guitars, Rosanne slips behind the grand piano on the altar and reviews the chord progressions of "I Was Watching You" from *Black Cadillac*. I've seen her warm up in this way before: at Gansevoort Street, where she brings herself into tune by communing with the small upright that stands against the wall. When she finishes, she pulls up her guitar from the stand and faces Andreas, and they listen to each other. Rosanne's wariness melts into warm acceptance. Much like newly introduced children who inevitably and immediately discern their mutual love of play, Rosanne and Andreas quickly find the artist in one another.

Clearly, he has done his homework, reproducing John's intricate licks from the wistful "House on the Lake" and the angry "Burn Down This Town," both culled from *Black Cadillac*. Rosanne zeros

Rosanne plays the piano while Danny confers with Andreas Binder.

in on his hands and seems ready to dance with the pompadoured guitarist. Danny, who's mostly negotiating with the sound and light people, eyes the budding relationship and smiles with satisfaction.

For the first time in Germany, the promoters have booked an opening act: a keyboard-led trio defined by dark, rolling chords and synthesizer embellishments. Repetitive rolling chords and lots of synthesizer embellishments. The lead singer and keyboard player, her hair bobbed like Prince Valiant's, wears a sparkly coat that she zips lower with each song until it is open, revealing a tight black shirt. Her sound claws at the senses, Enya with an edge. And if the audience needs a reminder that it is sitting in church, her chanting performance could bring to mind Gregorian monks.

Soon, the audience squirms. The one or two black cowboy hats I see stand up and go for beer. Others converse, giggle, fight sleep, and

Backstage with Andreas.

scan the church's ornate detail. One of the band's songs repeats, "vo, vo." Sounds to me like "go." They go. And make way for Rosanne.

While the band clears its instruments, the sound crew moves microphones into place for Rosanne. When Danny tapes the set list to the floor at the foot of Rosanne's mic stand, it's like dropping a glob of honey around bears. A few fans bolt to the stage to photograph it and no doubt contemplate how they will swipe it when the show ends.

I climb the creaking wooden steps to a side balcony and find a space next to a couple who smile reservedly when I sit. The husband tells me they are from the former East Germany, and today they have ventured to Berlin for only the fourth time since the wall came down in 1989. They spent the day in town and chose to cap their brief holiday with Rosanne, who they confess is an obscure name to them.

They came tonight because they know Johnny Cash—the same story I heard in Munich when I met the British expatriates.

From my new perch, I watch Danny stroll to the soundboard in the back and quietly pick up a microphone. "Ladies and gentlemen," he announces in a voice that harks to his days in radio, "for the first time in Berlin, please welcome Rosanne Cash." In front, Rosanne—dressed in the black brocade of Zurich—makes her way to the piano and summons the melancholy chords of "I Was Watching You." So, in the hours before showtime, she wasn't just going through the motions of a warm-up routine. She was preparing for the heart-wrenching, otherworldly meditation on young love, abandonment, and death. *And I was watching you from above / Because long before life there was love.*

On the heels of the keyboard-laden opening act, Rosanne in one moment proves to be the most soulful pianist to appear this night. But when "I Was Watching You" fades to silence, she walks away from the piano and never returns. She transitions to guitar and delves into "Dance with the Tiger," a cut from *Interiors* cowritten with folk music legend John Stewart that in Cologne was requested and rejected. *In every woman and man lies the seed of the fear / Of just how alone are all who live here.* She has barely touched *Interiors* on this tour, yet now it cuts the groove that she will inhabit throughout the entire concert. Perhaps the *Interiors* conversation in the car on the way to Essen inspired the choice, or the need to prove to herself that she can deliver "Dance with the Tiger" when she wasn't so sure in Cologne. In any event, the crowd welcomes it. I glance to my right to see my new friends holding hands.

A different performance emerges this evening. In John's absence, new space confronts her, so she works hard to fill it by plying her own strengths, particularly her songwriting. Her lyrics seem to realize a greater poignancy, their meaning more urgent, without the dynamic instrumental performance John provides.

The Berlin playlist.

Charged with fanning the dynamism all on her own, she calls on a surprise guest: a Berlin-based percussionist named Earl Harvin, with whom she had performed at the inspirational "Century of Song" festival in the fall. Four songs into the set—before she introduces Andreas —Earl trots onstage to a small kit that is just to her side. On "What We Really Want," a moody, loping number again from *Interiors*, he adds a depth and interest that John might have achieved on his bass strings. And he does it with short dreadlocks flying and broad shoulders grooving. "It's great to have a sexy man onstage," exclaims Rosanne. "And one who can play drums."

Berlin cheers. They get her English and dig her inclusion of Earl. Then she makes way for Andreas. She beams as he strolls onstage, and when he plays, she courts him, cradling her own guitar and jamming with him. In a way, the two equal one John. It doesn't hurt that Andreas, thrilled to be onstage with pop music royalty, is clearly trying to please Rosanne. He sprays flaming licks, inspiring Rosanne to wring all that she can from her guitar playing, which even she admits is limited.

Andreas and Earl hop on board "Runaway Train," which is more motor than mystery tonight. "Sehr gut?" she asks when it rumbles to a stop. And Berlin cheers.

Alone again, she rolls out "The Wheel," which never got a chance in Cologne, and "Blue Moon with Heartache," which becomes a fresco that could find a place on the walls of Passionskirche. Interestingly, the regular set makes no room for songs from *The List*. They crop up during the encore period, which is punctuated with that German applause that rises in determined unison, unlike the cacophonous American brand. To say good-bye, Rosanne gives them "500 Miles" and "Big River" and then, departing again from *The List*, sings them home to their beds and sleep with "Wouldn't It Be Loverly" from *My Fair Lady*. In the roar that greets her closing number, every other show from this tour seems years ago. She has filled her moment with creativity and élan.

When the house lights spread throughout the church, my neighbors on the bench turn to me, smiling. "She is a musician, a professional," the husband says. "She brings to Berlin a part of your culture. Another culture we don't hear about."

In the wake of this triumphant concert, Rosanne's mind swirls with impressions. "I felt great," she says. "I felt liberated, not from John by any means, but from any kind of darkness that surrounded the songs from *Black Cadillac* and also any kind of emotional complexity that surrounded *The List*. For some reason it just all congealed. . . . It was incredibly liberating. Maybe it just took me doing a lot of that by myself. Just to really own it and free myself of it at the same time. If that's not too precious.

"I don't know how to explain those types of things when the dots just connect and you realize why you are there and what you are doing and why it works and there's something about being in Berlin. The whole thing just resonated for me: past, future, present. And the audience was great, and it was like they had been waiting for me, and that's what the promoter told me afterwards, he said, 'They've been waiting for you.' So it was exciting.

"It's interesting. I felt like I was planting seeds for the future and at the same time reconnecting with the past. That's what I meant about how this thing came together. I don't really know why. I just felt the past coming up like this promise delivered to my twenty-year-old self that started in Germany and then at the same time planting seeds for the future. So it was a powerful week for me, really powerful. Really emotional. I mean, some nights I just wept after the show, like, 'Wow, this is different. This isn't just a gig.'"

Although Scotland is the coda in this European trip, it is also a homecoming, like Munich or the experience of traipsing through the repertory of *The List*. The Cash family's roots stretch back to the kingdom of Fife near Edinburgh, a fact that Johnny Cash realized on a plane ride when he sat next to a native of Fife who told him that the Cash name ran through most villages around his home. Cash had assumed his heritage was Irish, but a genealogist whom he employed to investigate his family tree confirmed what he had learned on the plane.

Ever since, Scotland has beckoned Rosanne. This woman whose childhood was torn by divorce and abandonment and dysfunction finds familial comfort in the country's ancient fields and towns. She inhales the air as if it were sweet lilac. She returns this time to tape an edition of the British Broadcasting Corporation's *Transatlantic Sessions*, a front porch–style jam session that brings together traditional

Taping *Transatlantic Sessions* with fiddler Aly Bain (l) and Jerry Douglas (r).

artists from America, Ireland, and Scotland. Dobro player Jerry Douglas regularly represents Nashville—as he will on this session—and over the years artists such as Kathy Mattea, Tim O'Brien, and Iris DeMent have joined him. Rosanne has visited previously during the show's long run.

This season's taping is housed in the hunting lodge of an old estate near Aberfeldy, the home of Dewar's Whisky and the legendary Black Watch regiment formed in the eighteenth century to thwart domestic crime and check foreign invaders. Over the previous weeks, various celebrity guests have cycled in and out of the tapings, including most recently James Taylor, who departed the day before Rosanne arrived. At the center of the show are Scotland's premier fiddler, Aly Bain, and accordionist Phil Cunningham, a jovial sort who may be Scotland's best-known emissary of traditional music.

"I've come back to this place that I love so much," she reflects within hours of landing in Scotland. "It is fraught with my ancestry, [this place] that I visited many times as a touchstone. And to play with these guys, Phil and Jerry and Aly. It moves me to play with these guys so much. To get into that Celtic flavor, Scottish flavor, to put that piece of the puzzle in. It's also like a homecoming. It's weird, isn't it? You don't usually get to do this kind of thing that has this big of a spiritual dimension. Usually you just go out and play a gig, but there is something about this that has a spiritual connection."

Rosanne and Danny arrive in Aberfeldy early in the afternoon on March 6. My plane arrives later, and when I figure out how to navigate my car away from Edinburgh, I head north to Aberfeldy in hopes of catching a bit of today's shooting. Zooming north on the left side of the M90 highway, I make it to town, check in at my hotel, and ask for directions to The Steading, which I believe to be the estate where Rosanne and her league-of-nations instrumentalists are performing. The hotel clerk prints directions for me, and I pull out onto the village's narrow streets and drive into the countryside. And farther into the countryside. The day is near its end, mist creeps onto the roadway, and for some reason I feel lost. Perhaps it's the passage of five miles with no road signs for Fortingall, where The Steading is supposedly located. I pass very closely by Loch Tay, where black water laps up on the nearby stony shore. Soon, I turn off the road and reexamine my directions. Just then, a station wagon comes to a stop beside me.

"You're lost," he calls in a thick brogue.

"Was I that obvious?" I tell him I'm looking for The Steading in Fortingall. "What Steading might that be? I live in a place called Steadings." And it is obviously not the place I'm seeking. He points me to Fortingall and tells me that I can't miss the hotel and to stop there and ask about my destination.

When I creep into Fortingall, I indeed see the white stucco facade of the Fortingall Hotel, glowing in the dusk. A smiling young woman points me about a half-mile back in the direction in which I had come and even describes the green door I should enter to find the taping. She's right. I walk right into the shoot. It's a good thing I'm not here to cause a disturbance because nobody knows me and nobody stops me.

Danny soon emerges from the set, and he leads me into an old stone-walled dining room with antler-accented chandeliers where Rosanne and the band are just wrapping up "500 Miles." Anxious to hear the take, the gang files into the control room, which is really the billiard room, and gathers around the soundboard, which is sitting on the billiard table. The engineer replays what may become *The List*'s featured song with its new British Isles inflections, and most everybody nods their approval. With the shaft of the night still free for dinner and drink, the hunting lodge evacuates.

Since the car rental agency in Edinburgh was out of the subcompact car I requested, I am driving a huge Audi station wagon. After the session breaks, I ask Rosanne if I can interview her about the German experience while it's still fresh in her mind. She suggests that we tape in my car while I drive her back to Aberfeldy town. Admittedly, the prospect of driving with Rosanne on the left side of the road horrifies me. I can read the headlines now: "Rosanne Cash Perishes in Scotland Crash." It's too close to the spirit of *The List*, the tragedy of country music, which has lost scores of performers in automobile catastrophes. If Rosanne had recorded Roy Acuff's "Wreck Along the Highway" for *The List* back in New York, I would have refused her a ride. Driving on the left side and attempting to conduct a taped interview? I don't recommend it. But I press forward, scraping left-side curbs and easing past oncoming vehicles.

Rosanne greets a pedestrian in Aberfeldy.

In the morning, Rosanne, who survived my interview on wheels and opted out of last night's whisky and lager, yearns to explore. She stops at churches and monuments and purveyors of tweed and gasps in wonder at every dell and castle and dark boiling river. Strolling in Aberfeldy town, she ducks into a tearoom and then lingers at the foot of a memorial statue to the Black Watch, absorbing every element of these scenes to store away until she returns again to Scotland.

In a gallery on the main street, she studies the paintings and block prints of the artist-proprietor, who seems to recognize his famous guest but can't quite place her. Rosanne won't help him, happy to maintain her anonymity in this quiet corner of the earth.

When she arrives for the afternoon taping in Fortingall, the set crackles like sparks in a Scottish hearth. While a loop of jigs and reels flows from the control room, musicians pop in and out of the great room, which is now a rehearsal space. As a cozy fire blazes and stag heads peer down, they work out an arrangement to another selection from *The List*: "Motherless Children." Old mandolin players and guitarists who will bely their age with riveting performances plug into laptops and MP3 players to absorb "Motherless Children," stored on an electronic file that Danny has sent to them. Jerry Douglas sits in a soft leather chair and rings out a few dobro licks that will accompany the classic. The drummer and bassist snooze on couches while crew members run in and out with lyric sheets and videographers capture outtakes for the broadcast.

In the dining room, Rosanne sits in a stylish mottled blouse taking pictures of Phil Cunningham, whose wavy white hair gleams. When the guitarists who have joined them get some traction with the song, Rosanne introduces them to her lyrical style. Three thousand miles away, John Leventhal's imprint shows. He has written a throbbing arrangement that thoroughly modernizes the song. It gives license to Jerry Douglas's red-hot dobro solo and a positively scintillating interjection of the flute.

They're almost ready to tape. A makeup artist touches up Rosanne, who shimmers under the intense light. Her finely combed hair radiates. In the great room, Aly Bain, whose fiddle is not called for on this take, tells Phil, who's also sidelined and preoccupied with card tricks, that "Motherless Children" shouldn't take long, it's sounding so smooth.

He's right. The song pulses. Rosanne's urgent vocals demand attention, and the men around her offer it. Their intensity rises. *Father will do the best that he can / But there are so many things he can't understand.* As if on cue, the small daughter of one of the female directors sobs as her sitter takes her away and into the afternoon that has become drenched with rain. The moment accentuates the

Visiting the site of an ancient yew tree in Fortingall.

elements of human sadness in "Motherless Children": familial loss, abandonment, and sibling betrayal. Like so many songs from the traditional canon, it pricks the emotions with the sparsest of verse, relying on our own intimacy with the human condition to flesh out its sentiment.

Aly slams shut the billiard room door so he can work on his part for the next set, but Rosanne and the band's "Motherless Children" overwhelms the oaken doors and ancient wall. It's as if *The List* is flexing its muscle. Soon, I crack open a paperback copy of a Steinbeck novel, nestle by the fire, and recline, surrounded by music. The Scottish kings should have lived so well.

In the blue dark of the Aberfeldy night, Rosanne's alarm bleats awake. I hear her in the room above me, stepping across the floor

from bed to bathroom, bathroom to closet. Her flight leaves Edinburgh earlier than mine, so I bury my head in the duvet and try to
doze off again.

Later in the morning I arrive in the departure hall of the airport
just in time to watch her Continental jet back away from the gate
and float toward the runway. Its silver wings shine in the country's
ethereal morning light.

CHAPTER 12

A Satisfied Mind

In the weeks after Europe, production on *The List* proceeds amid peril. Mike Bailey at Manhattan Records has been laid off, not for trying to erase the "Minnesota" lyric from "Big River" but as part of the massive wave of downsizing in the recording industry. Soon after, the record company suggests to Danny Kahn that *The List* might be better served on the well-known folk label Vanguard, which EMI distributes globally but does not own. Danny and Rosanne blanch, preferring to ride with Manhattan, which in early April has not one title on *Billboard*'s listing of the top one hundred albums.

News about the fate of the compact disc, and by extension the fate of the album, continues to shake the industry. Since New Year's Day, dozens of big-box store music retailers have shuttered their doors, while others on the edge of bankruptcy cut floor space dedicated to the compact disc. In March, *Rolling Stone* reports that more than thirty music stores have closed their doors since the beginning of 2009.

And still Johnny Cash's list is nowhere to be found, even after a few additional expeditions into the recesses of her upper room. Another psychic she has hired envisions the document pressed between book pages. But Rosanne fails to put her finger on such a book. Not that it matters much. The search for the spirit of southern music continues without the hard-copy map. The map is in Rosanne's mind, and it's led her to the sweet cream of country music: "She's Got You," "Silver Wings," "Bury Me Under the Weeping Willow," "Long Black Veil," "I'm Movin' On," "500 Miles," "Take These Chains from My Heart," and others. It's unknown at this point which ones will make the final cut.

By mid-April, though, she and John have stripped the album of "Big River," "Satisfied Mind," "Sweet Memories," and "I'll Be There." Most of Rosanne's vocals are recorded, and the instrumental tracks are virtually finished. For fun, she plans to ask Elvis Costello, Neko Case, Chris Thile, Jeff Tweedy of Wilco, Bruce Springsteen, and Rufus Wainwright to chime in on a few songs. Late spring also promises a full schedule of mixing, photo shoots, pre-release press interviews, clearances of copyrights for each song, and—maybe—planning for a fall tour.

Returning to New York one more time as production on *The List* wanes, I wish I could say that columns of warm spring air greet me. But as I emerge from the Ninth Street subway station, an insistent wind pushes me back like an invisible hand. Aboveground, raw April chill subdues New York, a reminder of the stinging winter just ended. Only the spring fashions lined up in shop windows promise easier temperatures ahead.

The sidewalks lead me to Gansevoort Street, where I know the last of the studio's recording equipment has been removed. Still, the knowledge that Rick and Craig's stuff safely traveled to new digs at West Twentieth Street does little to prepare me for the sight of a steel curtain pulled over 66 Gansevoort Street. Empty chip bags and cigarette packs swirl like small twisters against the cold gray exterior wall. And the woman in the mural who noted each coming and going has disappeared, suffocated beneath a coat of paint as red as blood.

Gansevoort Street in April 2009.

I hurry uptown to Chelsea, passing a few empty store windows and a surprising number of construction sites. I note one more time the antique stores and the doggie sitters and the restaurants named Klee and Buddakan as well as the shops with $5 coffee and the bars with $8 beers. Making it as far as West Twenty-third Street, I turn off Ninth Avenue and hustle past the Chelsea Hotel. One cold day in January, Rosanne visited a notary public across the street from the hotel where she—bundled from neck to knee against the offensive temperatures— brought the signed papers that would settle her father's estate. I glance over at the nondescript storefront and wonder how she felt that day. Knowing that her father's affairs were closing must have dammed another channel to him, but she seemed more resigned than sad.

Finally, I approach Rosanne's home. Two violet hydrangeas set down in pots at the top of her steps enliven her street like Chinese lanterns in the night. Those who pass can't miss the small spectacle. Even after several months of visits, my lungs sharply contract as I open the gate and start up the stairs. I have an uncomfortable agenda in mind. At no time during the days with her in Europe, on Gansevoort Street, or in her home have I engaged her in a substantial discussion of her father's interplay with her new album project. The icy stare from our Folsom Prison interview so long ago haunts me, as do newspaper and magazine interviews in which she fights to distinguish herself from her father and fend off charges of exploitation. I tried to have this conversation in February—before Europe—but she uncorked dramatic and tearful memories of her first encounter with Germany and recording. Her story magnetized me, but it delayed an inevitable conversation.

Indeed, she has dwelled on the list as inheritance and acknowledged the requirement to pass it to another generation, the burden of the balladeer. But, apart from that, I'm not sure how she connects to her father at this moment when his list and her *List* are mingling.

So I breathe deeply and rap on the door.

In the upper room, Rosanne and John have constructed new shelving for Jake's toys and her stuff. Displaced ledgers, books, picture frames, photo albums, and compact discs wait on the floor for relocation. They are for now arranged in stacks that block a path to more shelves jammed with boxes and master tapes.

Rosanne pulls a wooden office chair from John's office nook and wedges another one among the stacks. We sit and I ask her to return to October when she predicted that her father's list would only appear when she felt that it would not be appropriated away from her. "I don't have that fear anymore," she says. "If I really examine myself, I don't have that. I feel now that if I found it, I could show it to people or not show it. Isn't that interesting? October, November, December, January, February, March. Yes, in five months I really changed my feelings about it. I think recording them and starting to do the songs live has helped me to take ownership."

Somewhere in these stacks the list remains hidden, despite Rosanne's new impulses of ownership. But by this point she has ceased to insist that it will appear, as she had to Danny and John on the train to Munich, and instead dwells on the good fortune of its absence. Without the speculation and the ersatz lists, she argues, she and John never would have mined the list's spirit. "We would have all just commented on it: 'Oh, look, isn't that nice, oh, that one's there.' But the exploration that not having the list caused was as important as finding it." It has helped her, she says, "think more deeply about the songs themselves, and why would that one be on the list and does it hold up, does it fall apart, why would he have chosen it, where was he in his life that that would have been important . . . and why not that one or that one and that one, like 'Detroit City' or '500 Miles.' Do you know what I mean? It's not just this dry thing that's from the past, but it's about the thinking that led to him making it. . . . It's been so rich. I'm glad I didn't find it before now because none of that would have happened. I would have just taken it and gone, 'Okay, that one, that one, that one,' instead of all this thought about tradition and passing something on and also my dad's state of mind."

This glimpse that the list or *The List* has provided into her father's thinking reminds me of the daughter of another famous artist: Julia Wright, whose father, Richard Wright, wrote the classic twentieth-century novel *Native Son*. Many daughters of famous men could have a knowing sisterly conversation with Rosanne, but Julia may have a special bond with her because in the weeks after her father's death in 1960 she found an unfinished manuscript on his writing desk. "It was almost like a long letter, unsubmitted except to a few loved ones, and now to me," wrote Julia. She hadn't known that her father was at work on a new novel because she lived apart from him, but as she digested the fiction she saw truth: his grief and attitudes toward her and other family members. "Reading the faulty, sketchy, sometimes

Zurich.

repetitive draft was an opening of a door for me back then, in 1960, because he was voicing words he could not bring himself to voice out loud to us—his family." The incomplete novel, *A Father's Law*, remained unpublished for almost fifty years. Might the long delay have been protection from appropriation?

A *Father's Law* opened a window for Julia Wright. As Rosanne and I continue to talk in the upper room, it's obvious that *The List* serves a somewhat identical purpose. "Well, one thing it's gotten me in touch with," she explains, "is that my dad's love of songs and his obsession with songs never changed. That never got old for him. It wasn't like an adolescent passion that faded as he got older. So that makes me love him even more because I still feel that way about songs. I'm moved to tears with Bobby Womack singing 'Across 110th Street' live, and Dad felt like that too, so that's something that I share with him, not just as another musician but in a familiar way. And then that territory where the [concentric] circles cross is the list. Because I may not feel that way about all the songs on his list, but there are some that I do feel that same kind of intensity about, and then I have my own separate list that maybe he wouldn't feel the same way about. But we both know the feeling. . . . It sounds like a cliché a little bit, or hokey, but I actually feel really close to my dad making this record. I do. I feel close to him making this record. He would be so happy that I was doing it."

Our conversation turns to old ground: *The List* as an endeavor in song preservation. "We are doing it," she says, "with the love of a daughter, the respect of an archivist, and the sensibility of a New Yorker." And she returns to the question of appropriation, listing items such as letters, guitars, and photos that—like the list—she will probably never hand over to a museum or share with writers. And then she counts off the intangibles immune from appropriation: "The love he gave me, the service he provided as a parent. Those things we assimilate . . . and they are yours forever, nobody can take those."

"I see it in Jake a little bit," she says of appropriation. "He doesn't like to go to my shows, and once I was doing a reading when he was really little, and he was choking back tears, and then he just ran across in front of the audience to throw himself in my lap. That kind of raw possessiveness. 'This is my parent. I can't share her with all these people.' And I think I felt that when I was little: 'This is my dad, I don't want everybody to look at him or know him. Or think he's one thing when I know him to be something else.' I wrote about that for Annie Leibovitz's book about music, about how at some point I realized I had to be magnanimous, that he had a larger mission and belonged to the world and all of that. So that doesn't mean it was easy or there were not points in my life later on that I

Transatlantic Sessions.

just felt that I didn't want to share. Right after he died, it was particularly hard. I had to really be disciplined about not looking at the newsstand, not turning on the TV. He was all over. Danny was great about saying no to a lot of things people wanted me to do for them to help them express their sorrow at losing my father, which I was not willing to do. But I don't feel that. I don't feel that kind of childlike territoriality at all. But I am just clear on the things that are mine that I don't want to share with the world."

The appropriation began long before he died, as far back as her childhood, but I wonder if the appropriation came and went like seasons. Did it depend on his popularity, the demand for him, for example? "No, his availability wasn't determined by success, it was determined by drug use. If he wasn't using, even when he was busy and as famous as he could possibly be, if he wasn't using, he was available and he was great. If he was using and nothing was going on, didn't matter, couldn't reach him."

Yet the period near the end of his life must have left some opportunity for collecting lost time, I venture.

"That was a really painful time because he was so sick and I felt so helpless to help him. He was in a lot of pain, and there was even a period when he couldn't walk, and that was just devastating to him. At the same time, it was that shift in power from parent to child that happens when your parent gets elderly and sick, and it was very sweet. He started to want things from me, depending on me to do this or ask me to do that for him, and that had never happened before.

"It was the weekend of the blackout in New York, so it was August 14, [2003], I think, and I was in Nashville, and we had to go back to New York, and he was going to come up later in the month for the MTV awards, and he was confused and thought I was staying another day, and I said, 'No, Dad. I have to leave this afternoon at five o'clock.' And he said, 'But I thought you were staying and having coffee with me in the morning.' I said, 'No, Dad, I've got to go back. But remember, you are coming up to New York.' And he said, 'Oh, yeah.' And I could see in his face that he didn't think he was coming to New York when he said that. And I just felt torn up leaving him. It was like leaving a four-year-old, really disappointed that I was leaving and kind of lost.

"So I got to the airport, and the flight was delayed and then canceled because of the blackout. And I called Dad from the airport, and I said, 'Dad, what does CNN say?' Because he always had CNN on if he was awake. He told me what was going on with the blackout, and I said, 'Well, I'm just going to wait here and see if I can get out.' My flight hadn't been canceled by then. And then I sat at the airport for a couple hours, three hours, and they canceled the flight, but they put me on one at six o'clock the next morning. And I thought about it, and I thought, 'I cannot drive to Hendersonville and then get back in a car at four AM to drive out for a six o'clock flight. I'm just going to stay in a hotel near the airport, but I'm not going to tell Dad because it will make him feel even worse.' So I didn't tell him I was staying near the airport, and I felt bad about that."

Rosanne carries so much regret from that time that it is tempting to look at *The List* as atonement. She inevitably turns from any redemptive moments linked to her father's demise to emotions painful and dark. As in the airport story, the trend reveals itself again when I ask if she ever approached him in search of resolution to long-held conflicts.

"No, it was happening anyway," she replies. "It did not need verbalization for either one of us. When you just asked that question, a picture came in my mind. It was in July, and they were filming [a documentary] about the Appalachians, and so I was at the house with Dad, and we were singing 'Forty Shades of Green.' I mean, he was sick, it was just two months before he died. But someone took a picture of us sitting next to each other in those two big armchairs, and Dad was looking off [in the distance], and I'm looking down. In our faces you could see that we both knew, you know. It would have been redundant and kind of cheap to talk about it. It was happening. We were sitting there singing 'Forty Shades of Green.' What more redemption do you need than for me to sing that song with him?

"I was caring for him. I got the crew out of there as quickly as possible. I said, 'Look, you can't stress him out. You have to do this quick. Okay, that's enough. Dad, you need to sit down.' I was trying to take care of him."

"A parent can't ask for more in his final days," I suggest.

"I didn't get to do it enough."

"But you did it."

"Not enough, not enough," she protests, pushing her opens hands against her eyes to stop the tears. "I did do it, but not enough. He

Aberfeldy.

had too many buffers. There were so many buffers around: all of the women who worked for him and the nurses and the doctors and this and that. It was too much."

"So, even then you couldn't get as close to him as you wanted to?"

"No, I had my time with him, you know. And I would go down. When June was dying, I was there twenty-four-seven. And after she died, then I started coming down every two to three weeks to be with him. He got up early, so I would make myself get up at four-thirty and go into his office to have coffee with him. And that was a great time, because the ladies wouldn't show up until six or six-thirty. So we had a couple hours together.

"First we would watch CNN, and then I would read to him. And in the afternoon I'd read to him more. He took several naps a day then, so we'd be reading or I'd sing to him, sing Carter Family songs to him. And watch CNN. And if Jake was with me, Jake would draw him a picture of a Power Ranger or something. Pretty cute. He'd say, 'Now, what is that?' 'Power Ranger, Grandpa. Power Ranger!' . . . If it wasn't too hot, we'd sit out [on the terrace].

"Did I tell you about the vultures? They roosted outside the kitchen window. The house was kind of on levels, and Dad would get mad at them. 'Get out of here, get out of here.' It happened after June died. It was truly creepy."

Thoughts about appropriation and regret open the door to the question I have hesitated to ask these long cold months. It's based on observations of Rosanne that stretch back to 2004 when I interviewed her for the first time. Whenever she offered a substantive anecdote about her father, the color of longing or a twinge of regret almost always appeared on her face, as if the conversation was taking her to an experience with her father that gave her only fleeting solace or satisfaction. Indeed, there were moments that she found completely gratifying, but she described them with an unbridled enthusiasm that suggested she craved more from his memory.

Ironically, a memory of her father's back—yes, his back—appears to deliver him to her in the greatest clarity. She described it in 2007. "If I think about my dad, that's one of the first images that comes up: his back spotlighted. And there was a palpable kind of energy between him and [the] audience. He was his best self onstage. And he took his problems to the stage. And he worked a lot of them out onstage. He had this very odd combination of . . . showmanship and generosity of spirit and good-naturedness coupled with this absolute lack of need to please anyone, but to just do what he did to the best of his ability. It was such an odd combination. You don't see it in many performers. It was perfect, like you never felt that he would go outside of himself to please you, and yet he wanted to. He liked you.

"Once in the nineties he was playing Carnegie Hall. I think it was the last time he played Carnegie Hall. And he asked me to sing 'I Still Miss Someone' with him. And I was really pissed off at him at the time. There was something that came up for me, something about my childhood, like, 'Why did you do this or you never explained this.' So I said, 'No, I don't want to.' And then he asked me again the next day. It was a few days before. And I said, 'Well, you know, I'm going to have a headache or something like that!' And he said, 'Okay.' He didn't really say much. So the day of the show we went to his hotel room, me and John and the kids. And he asked me again. It was the third time. 'You sure you don't want to come up and sing "I Still Miss Someone"?' I said, 'I don't think so, Dad. I'm just not feeling up to it.' And he turned, and he walked out of the room. And it was his back. It was the look of his back. And so I said, 'Dad, I'll do it. Come back!' The great thing about doing it, about singing that song with him is that whatever I was angry about, whatever kind of rock was in between us, just dissolved onstage where he worked it all out. . . . It was the safest way he knew of fixing a relationship! Or starting one. He asked June to marry him onstage."

As I face her in the upper room, I suspect she yearns for more than the image of his back, that, in plain terms, she's searching for her father. "I don't like to hear that, but it's probably true," she confesses. "I was really close to my dad when I was really small, and I felt . . . not just it's your daddy and you're a little girl with your daddy . . . but I felt a resonance with him like he understood me and he really got me and I understood him. And then he came back from tour once when I was six or seven years old, and it wasn't him. So that sense of loss is in there. You know he got clean and sober, and I know that he loved me, and we spent time together. And even through the end of his life, when I was a grown, middle-aged woman myself, and even through all of that, there's still that moment, that imprint of six, seven years old of what happened to him. He disappeared. I'm sure some part of my psyche is trying to make restitution. All this time. You know, truthfully, a lot of the stuff about being magnanimous and sharing and knowing he belonged to the world is intellectual soothing."

She pauses, patting her tears, looking down at the piles of memories on the floor. "But I'm not broken, and I don't want to be broken about it, you know what I mean? That kind of public woundedness doesn't appeal to me at all."

She embraces the notion when I bring it up that *The List* may be part of the search for magnanimity and sharing and him.

"Yes, not just part," she says. "It's most of the reconnection. At this point, with my dad dead, it's all of the reconnection."

Will she always search for her father in her repertoire? My thoughts flow to *Black Cadillac*, and I recite a verse of "The World Unseen": *I will look for you in Memphis and the miles between / I will look for you in morphine and in dreams / I will look for you in the rhythm of my bloodstream.*

A smile cuts across Rosanne's face. "That's a good verse.

"I'm going to look for you in the list," she says, exhaling and looking to her side. "Of course, of course. . . . There is part of my destiny, my repertoire, which is just mine and his. But where they converge are the traits you pass down, the eyes, the hair, the songs on the list. I think I'll get this record done without finding it, though. I think that's probably good.

"This whole life around the list has gotten really rich and interesting, and the way John's been drawn into it too, it's a great point in our marriage, a great meeting place for us. He reinvented the way we play 'Sea of Heartbreak.' It makes me cry to think about it. He played it for me last night; he'd been working on it for two days. He'd

At Folsom Prison, 1968.

been really unhappy with the way we did it, and I was too. So he had this flash of a way to redo it, and he brought it home, and he was so excited when he got home and played it for me last night, and I put my hand on his arm, and I said, 'It's so good that it sounds like it's always been there.' And it did. That's kind of the point of the whole record, right? It feels so good that it's like it's always been there."

As I walk down the steps for the last time, a yellow bus slows in the street. Its door opens, and out leaps Jake, in an oversized white shirt, home from touch football. He bounds through the gate, charges up toward his mother for a quick hug before he slips past her like a running back evading a tackler. As I close the gate and step onto the sidewalk, I hear Rosanne laugh. I turn around and look up to see her framed by her vibrant hydrangeas, her clay-red steps, and her deep brown doorway.

Rosanne waves. Her eyes, like dark pebbles on wet sand, peer down the stairs. Her probing smile sails past me to summer.

ROSANNE CASH
The List

01	03:12	MISS THE MISSISSIPPI AND YOU
02	03:06	MOTHERLESS CHILDREN
03	03:06	SEA OF HEARTBREAK (W/ BRUCE SPRINGSTEEN)
04	03:32	TAKE THESE CHAINS FROM MY HEART
05	03:45	I'M MOVIN ON
06	03:21	HEARTACHES BY THE NUMBER (W/ ELVIS COSTELLO)
07	03:04	500 MILES
08	03:10	THE LONG BLACK VEIL (W/ JEFF TWEEDY)
09	03:07	SHE'S GOT YOU
10	03:33	GIRL FROM THE NORTH COUNTRY
11	03:42	SILVER WINGS (W/ RUFUS WAINWRIGHT)
12	03:34	BURY ME UNDER THE WEEPING WILLOW
	40:21	TOTAL OF PROGRAM

Notes

All quotes by Rosanne Cash and Danny Kahn are taken from the author's interviews with them, unless otherwise noted.

Chapter One: Movin' On

2   "He belonged to more than me": Annie Leibovitz, *American Music* (New York: Random House, 2003), 78.

2   "He makes good music": Laura Eipper, "Don't Label Rosanne Cash," *Country Music* (October 1980).

3   "He gives me advice": Ibid.

6   In a *New York Times* column: Rosanne Cash, "Well Actually It Is Brain Surgery," *New York Times*, April 5, 2008, available at: http://measureformeasure.blogs.nytimes.com/2008/04/05/well-actually-it-is-brain-surgery.

Chapter Two: Sweet Memories

35   Doubt it, although in letters home: Vivian Cash, with Ann Sharpsteen, *I Walked the Line: My Life with Johnny* (New York: Scribner, 2007), 175.

Chapter Three: Heartaches by the Number

40   While Rosanne records demos: "The Music Biz's Long Decline," *Rolling Stone* (February 5, 2009).

40   Winners this year: Ben Sisario, "Grammy's Golden Touch Loses
     Some of Its Luster," New York Times, February 19, 2009.

41   In early 2009, Pink Floyd's Dark Side of the Moon: Steve Knopper,
     "Digital Album Prices Slashed," Rolling Stone (February 5, 2009).

42   two U2 concert tickets: James Reed, "Sound Off: On Our Minds
     and on Our Playlists," Boston Globe, April 3, 2009.

44   "Rosanne Cash became": Jan Hoffman, "Some Girls Do," Village
     Voice, July 5, 1988.

44   "Cash was the rare writer": Geoffrey Himes, "Rodney & Rosanne:
     Are In-Laws Really Outlaws?" August 15, 2008, available at:
     http://www.sonicboomers.com/onthecorner/rodney-rosanne-are
     -laws-really-outlaws.

46   "That's how I first noticed her": Lloyd Sachs, "The Long Journey
     Home," No Depression (March–April 2003).

46   "Cash's sound is at its fullest": Vladimir Bogdanov, Chris Woodstra,
     and Stephen Thomas Erlewine, All Music Guide to Country: The
     Definitive Guide to Country Music, 2nd ed. (San Francisco: Back-
     beat Books, 2003), 138.

48   "I get lulled into thinking": Rosanne Cash, "The Not So Grand
     Tour," New York (June 29–July 6, 1998).

50   The album, she said in 1993: Roger Catlin, "Cash, Divorced from
     Nashville and Husband, Tries New Life," Hartford Courant, June
     16, 1993.

50   "Interiors flies in the face": Wayne King, review of Interiors, Rolling
     Stone (November 15, 1990).

50   Joel Selvin of the San Francisco Chronicle: Joel Selvin, "Rosanne
     Cashes in on Her Humanity," San Francisco Chronicle, December
     17, 1990.

52   "The Wheel is about": Steve Pick, "Rosanne Cash: A Perfect Chron-
     icler of Broken Hearts," St. Louis Post-Dispatch, April 2, 1993.

53   At the time, one journalistic wag: Jim Washburn, "Cash, Crowell:
     Two Stars Pass in Lyrical Night of Lost Love," Los Angeles Times,
     August 3, 1994.

54   "Instead of sounding like": Geoffrey Himes, review of *10 Song Demo, Rolling Stone* (May 2, 1996).

Chapter Four: Sweeter Memories

59   Box stores that are a more familiar sight: Federal Writers' Project, *The WPA Guide to New York City* (New York: Random House, 1939), 153.

74   And those who still search: Jeremy McCarter, "America in Harmony," *Newsweek* (April 13, 2009).

Chapter Five: Big River

79   "Patsy Cline was wicked": Rosanne Cash, "Patsy Cline: Honky-Tonk Angel," *New York Times Magazine* (November 24, 1996).

88   In 1998 she contributed: John Harvey, ed., *Blue Lightning* (London: Slow Dancer Press, 1998), 23–39.

Chapter Seven: Miss the Mississippi and You

112   "I'm reluctant about getting caught up": Hawkeye Hurst, "Rosanne Cash Makes Stardom Wait Its Turn," *Orlando Sentinel*, March 23, 1986.

112   "I just don't enjoy": Steve Morse, "Rosanne Won't Walk the Nashville Line," *Boston Globe*, November 19, 1987.

112   "Well, you know, there's a formula": Alanna Nash, *Behind Closed Doors: Talking with the Legends of Country Music* (New York: Alfred A. Knopf, 1988), 58.

Chapter Eight: Silver Wings

125   And Zurich is clean: Rosanne Cash, "The Not So Grand Tour," *New York* (June 29–July 6, 1998).

128   A decade ago, Rosanne wrote: Ibid.

Chapter Nine: Five Hundred Miles Away

141   "The roots of my longing": Annie Leibovitz, *American Music* (New York: Random House, 2003), 79.

Chapter Ten: Take These Chains

158   Not surprisingly, somebody: Alanna Nash, *The Very Best of Rosanne Cash* (Sony BMG Music Entertainment, 2005).

160   Rosanne's German fans: Mezz Mezzrow, with Bernard Wolfe, *Really the Blues* (London: Flamingo, 1993), 196.

162   Whether Rosanne knows it or not: Joe Smith, *Off the Record: An Oral History of Popular Music* (New York: Warner Books, 1988), 1.

Chapter Twelve: A Satisfied Mind

187   News about the fate of the compact disc: Steve Knopper, "Tanking CD Sales Shutter Stores," *Rolling Stone* (March 19, 2009).

191   "It was almost like a long letter": Richard Wright, *A Father's Law* (New York: Harper Perennial, 2008), vii.

Bibliography

Reference

Bogdanov, Vladimir, Chris Woodstra, and Steve Erlewine, eds. *All Music Guide to Country*, 2nd ed. San Francisco: Backbeat Books, 2003.

Bufwack, Mary A., and Robert K. Oermann. *Finding Her Voice: Women in Country Music, 1800–2000*. Nashville: Vanderbilt University Press/ Country Music Foundation Press, 2003.

Burns, Ric, James Sanders, and Lisa Ades. *New York: An Illustrated History*. New York: Alfred A. Knopf, 1999.

Burrows, Edwin G., and Mike Wallace. *Gotham: A History of New York City to 1898*. New York: Oxford University Press, 1999.

Cantwell, David, and Bill Friskics-Warren. *Heartaches by the Number: Country Music's 500 Greatest Singles*. Nashville: Vanderbilt University Press/Country Music Foundation Press, 2003.

Collins, Ace. *The Stories Behind Country Music's All-Time Greatest 100 Songs*. New York: Boulevard Books, 1996.

Federal Writers' Project. *The WPA Guide to New York City*. New York: Random House, 1939.

Jackson, Kenneth T., ed. *The Encyclopedia of New York*. New Haven, Conn.: Yale University Press, 1995.

Kingsbury, Paul, ed. *The Encyclopedia of Country Music*. New York: Oxford University Press, 1998.

Kingsbury, Paul, and Alanna Nash, eds. *Will the Circle Be Unbroken: Country Music in America*. New York: Dorling Kindersley, 2006.

Leadbitter, Mike, Leslie Fancourt, and Paul Pelletier. *Blues Records 1943–1970*, vol. 2. London: Record Information Services, 1994.

McCloud, Barry, ed. *Definitive Country: The Ultimate Encyclopedia of Country Music and Its Performers*. New York: Perigree, 1995.

Meade, Guthrie T., Jr., with Dick Spottswood and Douglas S. Meade. *Country Music Sources: A Biblio-Discography of Commercially Recorded Country Music*. Chapel Hill: University of North Carolina Press, 2002.

Sanjek, Russell (updated by David Sanjek). *Pennies from Heaven: The American Popular Music Business in the Twentieth Century*. New York: Da Capo Press, 1996.

Smith, John L. *The Johnny Cash Discography*. Westport, Conn.: Greenwood Press, 1985.

———. *The Johnny Cash Discography, 1984–1993*. Westport, Conn.: Greenwood Press, 1994.

Whitburn, Joel. *Top Country Albums, 1964–1997*. Menomonee Falls, Wisc.: Record Research, 1997.

———. *Top Country Singles, 1994–1993*. Menomonee Falls, Wisc.: Record Research, 1994.

———. *Top Pop Singles, 1955–1993*. Menomonee Falls, Wisc.: Record Research, 1994.

General

Brown, Cecil. *Stagolee Shot Billy*. Cambridge, Mass.: Harvard University Press, 2003.

Cash, Johnny, with Patrick Carr. *Cash: The Autobiography*. San Francisco: Harper San Francisco, 1997.

Cash, Rosanne. *Bodies of Water*. New York: Hyperion, 1996.

———, ed. *Songs Without Rhyme: Prose by Celebrated Songwriters*. New York: Hyperion, 2001.

Cash, Vivian, with Ann Sharpsteen. *I Walked the Line: My Life with Johnny*. New York: Scribner, 2007.

Coleman, Mark. *Playback: From the Victrola to MP3, 100 Years of Music, Machines, and Money*. New York: Da Capo Press, 2003.

Escot, Colin. *Lost Highway: The True Story of Country Music*. Washington, D.C.: Smithsonian Books, 2003.

Harvey, John, ed. *Blue Lightning*. London: Slow Dancer Press, 1998.

Jones, Margaret. *Patsy: The Life and Times of Patsy Cline*. New York: Harper Collins, 1994.

Leibovitz, Annie. *American Music*. New York: Random House, 2003.

Mezzrow, Mezz, with Bernard Wolfe. *Really the Blues*. London: Flamingo, 1993.

Nash, Alanna. *Behind Closed Doors: Talking with the Legends of Country Music*. New York: Alfred A. Knopf, 1988.

Porterfield, Nolan. *Jimmie Rodgers: The Life and Times of America's Blue Yodeler*. Urbana: University of Illinois Press, 1979.

Self, Philip. *Guitar Pull: Conversations with Country Music's Legendary Songwriters*. Nashville: Cypress Moon Press, 2002.

Smith, Joe. *Off the Record: An Oral History of Popular Music*. New York: Warner Books, 1988.

Tosches, Nick. *Where Dead Voices Gather*. Boston: Little, Brown, 2001.

Wilentz, Sean, and Greil Marcus. *The Rose and the Briar: Death, Love, and Liberty in the American Ballad*. New York: W. W. Norton and Co., 2005.

Wolfe, Charles. *Classic Country: Legends of Country Music*. New York: Routledge, 2001.

Wolfe, Charles, and James E. Akenson, eds. *The Women of Country Music: A Reader*. Lexington: The University of Kentucky Press, 2003.

Yetnikoff, Walter, with David Ritz. *Howling at the Moon: The Odyssey of a Monstrous Music Mogul in an Age of Excess*. New York: Broadway Books, 2004.

Zollo, Paul. *Songwriters on Songwriting*, 4th ed. New York: Da Capo Press, 2003.

Zwonitzer, Mark, with Charles Hirshberg. *Will You Miss Me When I'm Gone: The Carter Family and Their Legacy in American Music*. New York: Simon & Schuster, 2002.

Album Liner Notes

DeCurtis, Anthony. *Interiors*. Sony BMG Music Entertainment, 2005.
Nash, Alanna. *The Very Best of Rosanne Cash*. Sony BMG Music Entertainment, 2005.

Photo Credits

With her father in London, 1975. Photo by Alexander Agor. Courtesy of the Rosanne Cash Collection.

1988. Courtesy of the Rosanne Cash Collection.

Recording *Right or Wrong* in Beverly Hills. Clockwise: Rosanne, drummer John Ware, guitarist Hank DeVito, Brad Hartman, Bronco Newcombe, and bassist Emory Gordy, Jr. Courtesy of the Rosanne Cash Collection.

Rodney Crowell and Rosanne, 1987. © Alan Mayor.

Rosanne in 1987. © Alan Mayor.

Rosanne in Memphis, circa 1990. Courtesy of the Rosanne Cash collection.

On the road for *The Wheel* with (l to r) John Leventhal and drummer Dennis McDermott. Courtesy of the Rosanne Cash Collection.

Rosanne with her father in 1988. © Alan Mayor.

Vivian and Johnny. Courtesy of the Rosanne Cash Collection.

Helen, Mother Maybelle, and June at Sunset Park in Pennsylvania, 1962. Photo by Leon Kagarise, © Pete's Pluckins.

Rosanne with (l to r) Loretta Lynn, Reba McEntire, and Holly Dunn in 1987. © Alan Mayor.

Rosanne in Renata Damm's apartment, 1978. Courtesy of the Rosanne Cash Collection.

At Folsom Prison, 1968. © Jim Marshall.

Index

215